MW00936036

Published by Spectrum, Inc.

21001 N. Tatum Blvd.
Suite 1630-472
Phoenix, AZ 85050
USA

ISBN: 1452855463

EAN-13 is 9781452855462

Library of Congress Control Number:

First Printing: May 2010

Dream to Destiny

By Dina Beauvais

Table of Contents

Dedication

Without my amazing husband Mark, this book would not have been possible. He has been 110% supportive. After doing the DreamTouch™ Questionnaire in Appendix A with Mark in early 2009, it became clear to both of us that his dreams and passions are in perfect alignment with the subject of this book. Thankfully, Mark became excited about this project and decided to utilize his gifts and talents to help make it a success.

"Dream to Destiny" is dedicated to my wonderful husband Mark and our 4 beautiful children – Daniel, Nicole, Lauren and Luke. May you always pursue your dreams by way of your gifts, talents and God-intended passions. Always strive to cultivate ALL your natural resources so that you may step into your divine destiny and become who you are designed to be.

All My Love – Dina (Didi and Mom)

Foreword

There is a fatal flaw in the books, movies and CD programs that teach about the law of attraction. Several important *keys* are missing. For this reason, many people who try to follow these programs fail miserably. I will share with you the **hidden keys** that, when applied, will help you manifest[1] dream after dream in your life like my clients and I have.

Since 1986 I have been living what I teach in this book. I practice what I preach. I went from being suicidal, as well as spiritually and emotionally bankrupt, to living a fulfilled life of abundance in a short amount of time after applying this method. For nearly 25 years I've been a tenacious student, practitioner and teacher of personal excellence, working hard to become my very best and help others do the same. One of my strengths is immediately applying things I learn and putting them into practice. As I did, new insights were gained. I have tested and experimented with many methods over the years. Those that worked, I kept. Those that didn't, I discarded. After many years of research, study and practice I created the method contained in this book.

Success

The greatest goal I've achieved is a well-balanced life of success. This was a lofty dream for me because I came from a life of zero balance and pure chaos.

What is "success" to you? In my view, far too many consider success the attainment of material wealth (money and possessions) or a high level of recognition in their field, usually accompanied by money and possessions. Material wealth does not equal success, and success does not equal material wealth.

I believe success is achieving a level of fulfillment, excellence and balance that fills your life with purpose, joy and a passion for what matters to you most. Our lives should also contribute to the greater good somehow. Wealth is not wrong and it is not bad, but wealth by itself does not measure success. A person might live on a very modest income, but if they love what they do, they can support themselves or their family and benefit their community, they can be very successful without material wealth.

Too often riches are accompanied by interpersonal disaster, family tragedy or emotional upheaval. You can have millions of dollars and possessions galore but be personally or morally bankrupt. Life lived this way misses the mark of success.

9

Ultimately, you must determine your priorities and what success means for you. To me, a successful life achieves excellence and balance emotionally, spiritually, physically, relationally and financially. My husband and I also want to benefit the common good, making a difference in the world around us. Achieving and maintaining this kind of balance is true wealth. These are the measures I strive for and how I determine success. Consider now what success means to you.

Mission and Purpose

My mission in writing this book is to share my method with you and teach you how to manifest new realities in your life during these challenging economic times (most agree the worst economic recession since the Great Depression). My purpose is to encourage you, lift you up and help you break out of the recession/depression mind set. No one has to be a victim of the economy, a victim of their upbringing or a victim of their circumstances. You can rise above current market conditions like my clients and I have after applying the method described here. You can rise above the recession by tapping into The 3 Powers™ simultaneously to make your dreams realities. You will learn to harness your power to your passion and soar like an eagle, rising above your circumstances. You will learn how to direct your thinking, replace negative behaviors with positive ones and unlock the creative genius in you. If you follow this method, you will learn to create opportunity right where you are by cultivating the goldmine within you. You may begin devising ways to CREATE jobs rather than ever having to look for a job again. This is what I did during two major recessions.

By following the method I will describe, I manifested the following dreams quickly by tapping into a Power greater than the universe:

- In 1989, at **age 22**, I earned the **President's Club award** as a top sales producer for a **Fortune 500** technology company within my first **11 months**.

- Since 1991 I have sold every condo, townhome or house I owned (eight total) in **less than 1 week** using this method.

- In 1992 I broke several long-standing bad habits within **two months**: Cigarette smoking, cursing, over drinking and negative thinking.

- In 1993 I manifested my dream husband into my life within **two months**.

- In 1994 I started a technology company from scratch and built it to a multi-million dollar cash business **within three years**.

- Between 2000 and 2003 I manifested my daughter and son **two years** apart.

- In 2009 The Los Angeles Times voted two of my patent pending products in the top three innovations created in the 2009 recession (within **three months** of applying for the patents).

- In 2009 I got a vision to share the Dream Program on national television. Within **two days** a TV producer from New York called and interviewed me on the spot. You will see us sharing parts of this program on prime time network TV[2] nationally and internationally over the next four years.

This is just a partial list of the many dreams I've manifested over the last 24 years applying The 3 Powers™ *simultaneously*. Because I live this program, I go after and achieve most everything that I strongly desire *fast* using this method. Many other stories of dreams realized are shared throughout to inspire you. It has worked for me, for many others and it *will work* for you too!

Trial & Error

Through trial, error and application I've perfected this process over the past two and a half decades, have applied for a method patent and began teaching it to others with great success. Many are now manifesting their dreams and desires using this method. They are stepping into their destiny and becoming who they are designed to be. They are finding their unique purpose in life – their niche. And they are much happier as a result. You can be too.

The secret is far greater than the law of attraction. This law is one small piece to the puzzle. Within these pages, you will learn to harness the powers available to you and apply them in your life, achieving miraculous results again and again. Give a person a fish and they will eat for a day. Teach a person how to fish and they will eat for a lifetime. I will teach you how to fish.

Reality TV

When our family was invited to appear on the hit Reality TV show **"Wife Swap"** (ABC Network, Lifetime Network, RDF Media), my husband and I were not familiar with it – we don't watch much television. The show's producer overnighted a DVD with two episodes for us to watch so we could learn more about the show. Our advisors told us "any publicity is good publicity" and that such broad exposure couldn't be bought at any price.

After careful thought, prayer and advice, we accepted the offer to be featured on our own episode. We thought it would be a terrific opportunity to share "Dream to Destiny" and the *Dream Program* (http://DreamProgram.com) on primetime national and international TV, since the show airs in 21 countries around the world. Our objective then, as it is now, was to bring a message of hope and encouragement to everyone – that your dreams can become your reality.

The very fact that we were going to *be* on national TV was a dream manifested in itself. We understood that anything could happen in terms of how they might portray us, but went into it with attitudes of faith and confidence. We knew if we were true to ourselves, it didn't matter how they depicted us because all things would work out for our good. We wanted to be genuine and we were. All in all, we are grateful we had an opportunity to be a part of the show.

Introduction

I want your Dreams to come true.

Dreams for a better life – physically, emotionally, financially, spiritually – are desires deeply rooted in the human heart. We are so fortunate to have the opportunity to choose the course of our lives. America was built by visionaries and dreamers. Our history is filled with their great success stories.

These dreamers and visionaries dared to follow their passions and dreams and truly believed that *anything is possible.* We must realize that this is more than an expression. It is a promise. It is the truth – *anything is possible!* However, in order for it to be true, we must have the vision and passion to turn our dreams into realities. Our history is full of examples that inspire and remind us of this.

- Abraham Lincoln dreamed of becoming president of the United States. He overcame great odds and persevered through many trials to achieve this dream. He ended the scourge of slavery and reunited a country torn by civil war at a defining moment in our nation's history, shaping our destiny.

- The inventions of Thomas Edison were huge technological advancements in our society that would not have happened without his passion and vision.

- The Wright brothers were told they would never fly – indeed, that man was not *meant* to fly – but they were not deterred. They dreamed of a flying machine and realized that dream, ushering in the era of air transportation.

- Henry Ford's vision of low-cost, reliable automobiles for everyone led to the mass-produced Model T, changing the face of transportation around the world. Few know of the consistent opposition and criticism he faced.

- After the Great Depression, Barron Hilton dreamed that his tiny hotel would one day grow to be a huge international hotel chain. Today, the Hilton name is one of the most recognized hotel brands in the world.

- Martin Luther King, Jr. had a dream of racial equality that changed the destiny of America. His passion drove him at the cost of his life. The story of Dr. King's peaceful struggle for racial equality is standard curriculum for American school children. He is honored in a manner similar to our greatest presidents.

Of course, these are the legendary stories most of us know. Many other examples could be cited. If you could speak to these individuals, each one would tell a familiar story. They would tell you that along the way there were many moments of doubt and near failure. They would stress the importance of perseverance. They would tell you of their passion for their vision. They might also share about the many people who thought they would never succeed. These "dream-stealers" and doubters, naysayers and critics are in everyone's life. They would also tell you that they *did not listen* to such people (many of whom were probably family members or relatives). Instead, they clung to their dreams and visions. They were driven by a passion that did not waiver. They reached the mountaintop. And when their victories or successes were celebrated, these very same people probably gathered around them saying, "We *knew* you could do it!"

Persevere

These dreamers and visionaries are no different than you or me. What history makes clear though, is that they took *action* in regards to their dreams with purpose and perseverance. They would not let their dreams slip from their hearts or minds. Because of this, their dreams became their realities and shaped their destinies. The same can be true for you!

The dreams, visions and passions of these legends were planted within them for a reason. They were there to benefit "the common good" – serving the greater good of humanity and the world around them. That may sound lofty, but when we function in the area of our gifts and talents (our natural resources), pursuing what we are passionate about, we make the world a better place. We improve the lives of others and the environment around us. This changes our world!

If we connect with that which is above us (God, our Higher Power), we tap into power greater than we possess on our own. On the contrary, if we attempt to go through life using our own power, we are likely to live a meager and frustrated existence.

Do Not Settle

Do not settle for a life of mediocrity or misery, doing something just for the money, or doing something you hate because it's what you know. We each have great potential and the possibility of a prosperous and fulfilling life. This does not mean riches (though that's possible), but a life filled with meaning, joy and purpose. But we must find this path and focus our thoughts in that direction. In this way we identify our destiny. "Dream to Destiny" will teach you how.

When we do what we are destined for in this world no one can stop us. However, we must run the race marked out for us with perseverance.[3] What is the race marked out for you? After reading and doing the exercises in this book, you will know what your race is, what your unique purpose in this life is. You will discover the *True Dreams* in your heart, and learn to manifest their reality. You are meant to live with passion and purpose. Ancient wisdom teaches that without dreams and passions, people slowly die emotionally, spiritually and physically.[4] Don't let this happen to you! You have the opportunity to live life to the fullest, live your dreams and live with passion. Don't settle for less.

You may find some of the ideas and concepts contained within this book radical or hard to accept. It may challenge your conventional thinking – personal, spiritual, religious or otherwise. If this is true, good! Embrace new forms of thought. Major shifts in life, our paradigms, character or behavior rarely happen in ways that are comfortable or easy. These concepts are not based on opinion, but on eternal truth, ancient wisdom and natural universal laws. All of the elements presented are things I have personally experienced. I practice and live these principles daily. That is why I am so confident in this system. It has worked consistently in my life for 24 years! This method has worked for others, and it will work for you too, as long as you do it!

What will your destiny be? What are your true dreams and passions? Imagination influences aspiration. All accomplishment begins with a vision and a dream. Your dreams determine your destiny. Without vision, passions die. Without vision, dreams fade. Without vision, destiny disappears. Without vision, people perish.[5]

Time for You

It is time for you to re-discover your dreams. It is time for you to identify your true passions. It is time for you to live the life you were designed to live. It is time for you to be the person you were created to be. It is time for you to become who you are meant to be. It is time for you to step into your destiny. Dream to Destiny will help you do just that!

Part I

The Gold Mine Within…

Your Natural Resources

Our world without is a reflection of our world within.

Chapter 1

My Story...

You become what you think about.

What you are about to read in the next few pages may seem dramatic or hard to believe. The reason I choose to share this with you is to show that I am living, breathing proof that anything is possible. My life is a miracle. Through a power far greater than my own, I changed the course of my **destiny**. It all started with a single dream...

I grew up in St. Louis, Missouri, the eldest of three girls. My parents divorced when I was seven after years of horrible fighting. Raised by a single mother who was diagnosed bipolar, Mom was in and out of institutions from the time I was five until I was 18 years old. She still tells me that we lived "below poverty level" on $800 per month for a family of four.

My dad was a doctor – a surgeon. He was quite successful, but the court-ordered child support for us was $800 per month, so that's all he paid. Dad remarried right away and started a new family, so that's where his attention went.

I was not raised with boundaries or structure. Seldom would anyone get me up for school, make breakfast for me or help pick out my clothes. I felt like I raised myself. When I was in second and third grade I did my best to help my younger sisters, but all they would do is fight and curse me, so I quit trying that.

Police were called to our house late at night for many different reasons. One night, in a drunken rage, my mom's boyfriend blew a hole through our front door with a shotgun; another time he rammed his car through our garage door. Inside there was yelling, screaming and physical fighting. There were holes in walls and doors. At one point I put a padlock on my bedroom door to keep everyone out. Most of my friends were not allowed to come to my house or even hang out with me.

During our short visits to dad's house we were left pretty much on our own there too. Dad was always working and our step-mom would be off by herself reading until we were gone — she wanted nothing to do with us. "Wild animals" is what my father and step-mom called us.

During the times Mom was in the hospital, we were passed around to relatives, neighbors or friends. Dad would take us for short periods, but he kept an extremely busy work schedule, so this wasn't really an option. At one point Dad won full custody of us three girls, but his wife threatened to divorce him if he kept us, so he sent us back to our mom. No one really *wanted* us, so as soon as mom came home from the hospital, back to her we'd go.

At age 13 I turned to alcohol and drugs to escape the pain of my life. The crowd I chose consisted of high school dropouts, stoners and drug dealers. This made things worse. Fortunately, I left this scene the following year.

Throughout high school I was consumed with self-destructive thoughts. I hated school and hated life. Tormented by depression and negative thoughts, at 18 I attempted suicide. I gave up on life. Thankfully I was unsuccessful. This really shook things up for me, but not in ways I expected. All of my close friends abandoned me. I felt like a social outcast. This desperate attempt was the manifestation of all my toxic thinking up to that point. Eventually I realized how selfish this was and *never* thought about suicide again.

The first 18 years of my life had enough drama and dysfunction to last a lifetime. My relationship model was a mess – angry divorced parents, abusive boyfriends and cold, unloving stepmothers. I never wanted to marry and *never* wanted children because of the misery handed down to me. I saw no way to break the chain of dysfunction. I thought, "Why bring a child into this messed up world?"

At age 19, while in college, I began to learn about the power of the mind (both conscious and subconscious) for the first time in my life. One of my professors taught us how to best study for exams. He told us to review our class notes and textbook highlights each night just before going to sleep so the material would sink into our subconscious minds faster and better due to our relaxed state. This is called "brain-based learning." This became a great habit I developed and put into practice daily. As a result I earned a 3.6 cumulative GPA upon graduating.

A short time later a friend introduced me to amazing books on the power of positive thinking. I began to learn about the power of my thoughts. He encouraged me to read great books like *Think and Grow Rich* by Napoleon Hill, *How to Win Friends and Influence People* by Dale Carnegie, *The One Minute Manager* by Ken Blanchard and many others. I became an avid reader, devouring books about taking control of my thinking and training my mind for success.

Looking back, I feel very fortunate and grateful for my childhood. It made me strong, self-motivated and determined. It prepared me to help others with similar struggles. It also drew me close to my

Heavenly Father, because most of the time he was all I had. Thankfully, my mother taught us about God. She often told us to "ask and it shall be given to you."[6] My mother and father did the best they knew how, because they each had very challenging upbringings themselves. Mom tells me she had *no one* to help or support her — family or friends. She says they often worked *against* her, which is why life was so challenging for her.

Turning things around in my life began with taking my thoughts captive and pointing them in the right direction. Most people *never* learn the importance of training their thinking, capturing negative thoughts and turning them into positives. I became a voracious student of the material I was learning, putting each new principle into practice. This new way of living was a great awakening at a pivotal time in my life. It set me on a bright new path. Pursuing my dreams, one passion and dream at a time, became the story of my new life.

Sunshine and Blue Sky Dreams

As college graduation approached, I dreamed of living in a climate filled with sunshine. I wanted to escape the dreary gray skies and bitter-cold winters of the Midwest. As someone who struggled with depression, I knew that blue skies and sunshine would be good for me. I learned to visualize the dreams in my mind using my imagination to bring them to life. Because I knew I could go anywhere I wanted, I literally studied an almanac to find the sunniest place in the country. A few weeks after graduating at age 22, I bought a one-way ticket to Phoenix, Arizona. The only person I knew in the entire state was my 89-year old Grandmother, who I wasn't close to. She was a part-time winter visitor there — a "Snowbird" as they're called.

I had three weeks before I knew I'd wear out my welcome with my Grandmother. So in 1989 during a major recession, I visualized the kind of high-powered position I wanted and landed my dream job with a Fortune 500 company within two weeks. Next I got a car. Then I got my own place. All of this happened very fast because my thinking was focused and I was taking *immediate* action.

The first few years in Phoenix were filled with hard work during the week and the party life on weekends. It looked like lots of fun on the surface, but it left me empty inside. I yearned for greater spiritual depth and meaning in my life. (You should know this about me — I love God! I have felt a connection with him since I was a little girl. In my most challenging times, I felt like the *only* one there for me was God. I am so grateful to him for that!)

I dreamed to break the chain of my past and have a normal, happy, healthy life with meaningful friendships, a loving relationship and success. I decided to use the method I was developing to break the chain of dysfunction handed down to me. Here are some examples of the dreams that manifested by God's power using this method:

- In 1986 I completely changed my body shape in **one month** from chunky and imbalanced to lean, strong and great physical condition. I've maintained this new physique for 2½ decades.

- Since 1991 I have sold every condo, townhome and house I owned (10 total) in **less than one week** using this method. In the 2008/2009 recession I sold 4 luxury homes within **four days**.

- In 1992 I broke several long-standing bad habits within **two months**: Cigarette smoking, cursing, over drinking and negative thinking.

- In 1993, through God, I manifested my dream husband into my life within **two months** by following this process.

- In 1994 I started a technology company from scratch and built it to a multi-million dollar business **within three years**, earning four-times what I had as a top producer for my former Fortune 500 employer.

- In 2000, after a devastating miscarriage, I manifested the daughter I dreamed of and a son **two years** later through the Power of God and prayer.

- In 2006 my husband and I built our dream home **in 15 months** in our dream neighborhood. We wanted a basement, two offices, a home gym and a family neighborhood with a community pool.

- In 2009 The Los Angeles Times voted two of my patent pending products in the top three "recession busters" created during the 2009 recession (within **three months** of applying for the patents).

- In 2009 as I was developing the Dream Program, I got a vision to share it on national television. The *next day* I received an e-mail with an invitation to appear on a primetime hit Reality TV show. Within **two days** I was speaking to a TV producer from New York about the show. We started filming a few months later.

These are just a few examples. There are many more. At age 25, when I decided to get serious about changing my life I wrote out positive affirmations to read and pray through every night before falling asleep and every morning upon waking.[7] This is a *very* important practice, which drives things deep into your subconscious mind. Here is a sample of some of the dreams that I read and prayed through each night and morning:

> *"I am very healthy and only eat foods that are good for me. I love my natural, sober state of mind. I am fit for life. I am very happy in my new church family where the people are truly loving and live out the Bible. I have several genuine friends who love me for who I am. I wait until I get married to have sex..."*

Closing my eyes, I would visualize and pray, meditating on these goals. This is how everything on the list above was accomplished. My subconscious mind was being programmed and my faith was being exercised as I tapped into the power of God to accomplish these goals. I visualized the desired results knowing that whatever my mind could conceive and believe it could achieve.

After diligently following the process described above for only one month, exactly what I dreamed was manifested. A kind lady I met at my doctor's office invited me to her church. I fell in love with it because the people were so loving and genuine and the teaching was straight from the Bible. It was the exact representation of my vision and now it had become my new reality. God was at work. Several women studied the Bible with me and my life was transformed from the inside out — heart, mind and soul.

There is a direct connection between training the mind and the truths contained in Scripture. Here's one example where Jesus states it very directly:

> *"If you believe, you will receive whatever you ask for in prayer."*
> <u>Matthew 21:22</u>

Immediately preceding this Jesus said, *"I tell you the truth..."* When the Son of God says, "I tell you the truth" we are well advised to pay attention.

A "Dream Job"

After living my transformed life for a few months, I began to dream of having my own company. I visualized and prayed to work from a home office and make several lifestyle changes. (This was way ahead of today's trend of corporate service executives working from home offices — it just wasn't done much then.) Within a few weeks a friend called and told me about an opportunity for me to stay in the technology industry, be self-employed and work from home while earning a full time income. Two months later I started my own company! Within three years I was earning four times the income working half the hours I had before. My dream became a reality!

During that time my schedule was built around the life I wanted. As my business ramped up, I chose to hire positive, energetic, spiritual people. It was wonderful! It grew to a multi-million dollar business in a few short years.

Miracles happen when you ask, believe and take action. The action I took was based on a growing faith. Prior successes gave me confidence. Like a muscle, faith grows stronger with use. I was also claiming the promises of God and calling on his faithfulness. If God says he'll do something, he will. Every time. You can count on that. If he says, "Ask and it will be given to you, seek and you will find, knock and the door will be opened to you," you can trust that. If he says, "I will always be with you..." or "I will never leave you or forsake you..." you can rely on that. We exercise and strengthen our *faith* when we take him at his Word. We can also take action with confidence and trust because he'll do as he promises.

My Dream Husband

I vividly remember the day I wrote out my ideal husband wish list. It was in the summer of 1992. In my journal I handwrote the following attributes I wanted in a husband: He has charisma, is a leader, a business person, my best friend, loves to work out, I'm attracted to him, a strong Christian, we're in love, he loves me unconditionally, etc. Then I prioritized these characteristics, closed my eyes and visualized my dream husband coming into my life. Once I got a vision of him in my mind, I prayed to be prepared to be an excellent wife.

Two months later Mark introduced himself to me at Beauvais' Gym while I was working out. This was my favorite health club and his brother was the owner. I had NO IDEA he was THE ONE. Interestingly, the third time we talked in the gym, Mark says that afterward he was overwhelmed with the strong and clear thought that he was going to marry me. (Isn't that amazing how Infinite Intelligence works? Mark was given a small vision of his future.) That day we had talked for about three hours, exchanged phone numbers and soon became best friends, one of the most important attributes on my list. We built an amazing friendship and were married a few years later.

Mark was everything on my wish list. We both decided to remain pure and save our physical relationship until marriage (yes, that really is possible). My dreams became my destiny!

Children?!

After being happily married our first year, I began to dream of having children. This was a *huge* transformation for me, because I *never* wanted children before, and I'd been telling myself that my entire life. Now I wanted it so badly I would cry. Becoming a mother became a burning desire. Tragically my first pregnancy ended in a miscarriage. This was very devastating, and took me months to recover from.

The only solution for me was to prepare my mind for a successful pregnancy. So I began to envision a healthy, happy baby girl with big brown eyes. To help my visualizing process, I cut out pictures of full-term pregnant women and healthy babies, focused on these pictures every night before I fell asleep and prayed with all my heart. My daughter Lauren was born 10 months later with big brown eyes. She was the exact representation of my visions, hopes and prayers. I was overjoyed and felt so very grateful that God had given me this incredible gift! Once again, my dream became a reality!

Fifteen months later my husband and I decided we wanted a second child so Lauren would have a sibling close in age to grow up with. Each night before I went to sleep I wrote out the following prayers: "Thank you, Lord, for giving Mark to me as my husband and Lauren as our daughter. Thank you for allowing me to get pregnant right away with a boy. Thank you that our son will be born full term, healthy and happy." I envisioned a little boy only because my husband wanted a boy. The idea of a son was very foreign to me because I'd grown up in a family of all women and had few, if any, examples of good men or boys in my life. (Truthfully, I thought most guys were jerks until I met my husband.) I followed the same mental process as before and gave birth to my son Luke nine months later. He was, *and still is*, so sweet! I absolutely adore him and am in love with him. I never knew boys could be so incredible. Another wonderful gift from God! Again, my dream became a reality!

Practicing What I Preach

In my naiveté I thought everyone did these things like I did. Over the last several years, I've learned that this is not the case. My faith is a gift. These exercises of faith (and manifesting) are strengths I've developed using my gifts. Because I know this method will help people, I want to share it. Your life can change to be anything you want it to be — *all things are possible for those who believe*. Do you believe that anything is possible? I do.

This process began for me in 1986 and I've been doing it successfully since then. It has worked for me time and time again.

Instead of going to school, learning an applied science, then "practicing" it on others, I learned it and practiced on myself. The guinea pig was ME! Then I tried it with my family. It worked for them too! Then I tried it with friends who were interested. It worked for them too. Then my husband and I taught this method to the other family on the Reality TV show "Wife Swap." We taught it in workshops and to our clients. It works for everyone who asks, believes and takes action!

Privately, I have been encouraging, sharing, training and coaching people on how to do these things for years. It started with family, then friends, then others who were referred to me. It grew. All along I was tweaking it to perfection. My goal was to encourage and help people the way I have been encouraged and helped. So I decided to organize it in a way that could be offered to others on a broad scale. I've seen nothing exactly like it, so I applied for a method patent (I'm an inventor anyway, so this made sense to me). Now the program has been formalized in this method. It worked for me. It worked for my family. It will work for you too, *if you do it*. It's that simple. The more you do it, the better you get at it.

Breaking the Chain

By the Power of God I was able to break the chain of depression and dysfunction handed down to me. He wants to do similar things for you. Throughout the book, I will share other examples of how I achieved dream after dream. Some took less than a week. Others were five years in the making. This is not just theory or something I believe in — I live it daily. Additionally, I'll share the stories of many others who have successfully manifested their dreams, visions and passions by putting these principles to work. These are only a few examples of *many* which could be shared. They have gone from dream to destiny and you can too!

My life has been a spiritual journey. I believe that's true for all of us. After all, we are spiritual beings living a human experience. For over two decades I have been very <u>diligent</u> about <u>visualizing</u> my most <u>passionate desires</u> and persistently <u>praying</u> (asking) for them with <u>faith</u> and confidence. The words underlined in the last sentence are very important. They are five of "The 7 Keys™" necessary to manifesting your dreams. We have each been given dreams and passions, gifts and talents, for a reason. The Almighty wants you to utilize and fully develop the gifts you've been given. You were meant for greatness, not mediocrity.

Maybe your unique purpose or niche in life is to be an excellent stay-at-home mom? Maybe it's to be a great teacher, a skilled carpenter, cook or CEO? Perhaps it's to be an artist, architect or athlete. It doesn't matter. Not everyone is an entrepreneur and it's not about becoming a millionaire. What's important is that you discover your True Dreams and Passions and connect them with the Gifts and Talents you were given at birth. In this way you will discover who you are designed to be. Then you can step into your divine destiny. The First Key is to get in touch with your True Dreams and Passions. Decide to believe in yourself. Know and understand that there is a Higher Power working in you and through you. Have the courage to pursue and realize your dreams. The 7 Keys™ shared in the "Manifesting Instructions" (Appendix B) give you clear and practical steps that, *if you do them*, will make your passions and dreams *come to life!*

Practical: Get a journal or notebook to use for recording your notes and thoughts. You will also use it for the different exercises in the book and appendices.

Start by answering these questions: What brought you to this place at this time? Is there a new direction you seek for your life? You've just read the story of how I broke the chain of dysfunction in my family. My husband broke the chains of alcoholism and abusive relationships. No chain is impossible to break. Is there a chain that you want to break? Write about these now.

Reality TV Bite: Stephen Key of InventRight (my invention mentor) is the one who initially contacted me about the opportunity to be on the primetime ABC hit Reality TV show "Wife Swap." He told me they were looking for inventor/entrepreneurs and that my husband and I should contact them because we fit the profile the show was looking for. After responding to the email Stephen sent me, the Wife Swap producers contacted us right away. That's how it began. We owe a *Great Big Thank You* to **Stephen Key** of **InventRight**. We are very grateful to you, Stephen!

Chapter 2

Discover Your True Dreams

"Follow your bliss and doors will open for you that were once walls."
— Joseph Campbell

What excites you? What motivates you? What moves your heart and gives you energy when you think about it, talk about it or do it? What do you daydream about? What do you wake up thinking about? These are some clues to your passions. These are clues to your dreams.

We are each special. Our passions, interests, deep desires, goals, visions and aspirations — these are what Dreams are made of.[8] The Dreams in our heart, along with our gifts and talents (the subject of our next chapter) are Key "natural resources" within us. Yours are different than mine. They are unique in each one of us. They are there for a reason. They are there by design, planted in you with a purpose.

As young children we had no trouble imagining BIG things! There was no limit to what we thought was possible — dragons, monsters, flying, invisibility, etc. We had BIG DREAMS! We thought nothing was impossible. As we get older, our wide-eyed wonder gradually dims, life begins to beat us up and beat us down. Our dreams shrink, our hopes fade and our imagination withers. Sometimes those responsible for this happening are the ones closest to us — parents, family members, teachers or friends. Before we realize it our dreams have died a slow, painful death. But it doesn't have to stay that way.

Get Reconnected

We need to reconnect with our dreams (most of us, anyway). We need to get back in touch with the childlike spirit we had as kids. Removing the "clamps" and "shackles" of limiting beliefs will allow our natural creativity and ideas to flow freely again. This is *imagination*. Then we can be free to dream BIG dreams once more and imagine limitless possibilities. If anything is truly possible, we need to let ourselves believe and act accordingly.

Your Dreams are shaped by your passions. Different things excite or motivate us individually. You're natural gifts and talents are practical clues to what you are intended to do. Our passions, gifts and talents are part of us for a reason. They are intended for use. You are meant to fully invest yourself in them. Why? Because you cannot be truly fulfilled in your life if your heart is not fully **in** what you are doing or what you're about.

To begin, it is vital that you identify, or get *in touch* with, your hidden dreams. This is the first Key and what we call DreamTouch™. This step is the *Key* to discovering your *True Dreams*. Notice I said "True Dreams"? These are not the dreams you *think* you should have, or think you're *supposed* to have. They are not the dreams *your parents* have for you, or your husband, your wife, etc. These are YOUR dreams — those that reside in the heart of your heart — the center of your mind. Getting in touch with your *True Dreams* will be nothing short of transformational.

You Might Be Surprised

We call this dream discovery exercise the DreamTouch Questionnaire (or "DTQ™" for short). The experience of conducting this exercise with our students and clients is amazing. In the matter of *one hour* most go from uncertain or disillusioned with their personal or professional direction, to knowing with clarity and vision what direction they want their life to take. It is incredible to see!

> "I was *very* skeptical at first, having been through several other attempts to discover my calling. I have to admit, though, that through Dina's unique DreamTouch Questionnaire, and especially the coaching session, she was able to draw out of my heart my true passions...which no one else has been able to do! Only **three months** after going through the Dream Program, I was offered a **miraculous promotion at work**. Thank you, Dina!!" Sean — San Diego, CA

I've seen this time and time again. Wouldn't you like to have this same sense of clarity? This is so important, because you cannot pursue your *True Dreams*, unless you *know what they are!* Most of our clients are surprised by what their true dreams actually are. This process often draws out desires they didn't even know were there, or helps them reconnect with dreams and aspirations they lost touch with long ago.

These dreams are often "hidden" because most people don't actually *know* what their *True Dreams* really are. Some do. You may be one of the lucky ones who are very centered on your dreams, passions and gifts, and you know it. If so, excellent! This method will still help you manifest those dreams into reality.

Others think they know what their dreams are, but after going through this soul-searching exercise, what they discover is often very different from what they first thought. Through the process our students and clients uncover dreams or passions that they lost touch with long ago, or didn't even realize were there — and they are amazed! Once you finish the DTQ, you will begin to experience a quantum shift in your life. Just becoming aware of your *True Dreams* sets the wheels of change in motion within you.

As mentioned earlier, the dreams, desires, passions, gifts and talents (natural resources) inside of us are there for a reason. They are there by design, intended for our good. When we identify them, recognize and accept them, not only do we understand ourselves much better, our very purpose begins to emerge. The picture of what our lives are intended to look like comes into focus. We begin to know with confidence that the life we truly desire is within our grasp. It is exciting!

What Gives You Energy?

To get an idea of where the DTQ will take you, ask yourself these questions:

> What gives me energy when I do it?
> What could I spend hours — day or night — doing and lose all track of time?

When I brainstormed these questions, I discovered several activities that really increase my energy and many of the answers surprised me. I love talking with positive people, playing with my children, working-out at the gym or outside and mentoring people through the Dream Program. I love being near the ocean, having long prayer-walks, taking time to read, relax and meditate. I love getting excited about new ideas or inventions, researching them and then following my God-given instincts to make them realities. These are just a few examples.

I choose to do all the activities that I enjoy doing and that give me energy. I do my best to delegate to others the activities that zap my energy such as cooking, cleaning and grocery shopping, for example. When doing the DreamTouch Questionnaire you will be asked to "Brainstorm all the activities that give you energy." This is very important because that which gives you energy is usually linked to your natural gifts and talents.

Imagine what life would be like if you and everyone else in the world lived with passion and chose professions based on what they loved, what they were gifted at and what gave them energy? Would our world be a better place? You bet it would!

When you are working, serving or functioning within your natural resources (dreams, passions, gifts and talents) you are positive and passionate. People are attracted to those who are positive and passionate. Passion persuades, passion sells and passion brings people back for more! On the other hand, people are repelled by those who are negative and miserable. These qualities drive people away. If you are *not* doing something you love, you will not be positive or passionate. You may even be negative and miserable. This is not where you want to end up. Don't settle for misery or mediocrity!

I urge you to take action and pursue your Dreams! Choose your profession and your life pursuits doing what you love, doing things that give you energy. Become who you are designed to be, who you are *meant* to be. Only then will you be able to step into your destiny.

Practical Steps

The Dream Program (www.DreamProgram.com) was created to take you from Dream to Destiny. It is a practical, patent-pending method that will teach you the very same things that have worked for me for the last 24 years. They will work for you too if you follow the steps. I call these steps "The 7 Keys™." These "Keys" are the practical steps that will be your roadmap for the journey from Dream to Destiny. The Keys will unlock the ability to manifest your Dreams, bringing them into your reality.

The DreamTouch Questionnaire (DTQ) exercise (Appendix A) will help you hone in on the healthy dreams within you.[9] Discovering your *True Dreams* is the first Key to manifesting your Dreams. You can't manifest them if you don't know what they are!

You are destined for *Greatness*, not mediocrity. The 7 Keys provide the roadmap that will guide you to your greatness. They are detailed in the "Manifesting Instructions" (Appendix B) and are the practical steps to go from Dream to Destiny.

WARNING! If you're anything like me, you're tempted to jump ahead and skip right to the Keys. ***Please avoid this temptation***. If you skip chapters or jump to the end, you will only be cheating yourself and missing vital information which will educate and help you. In fact, even the **Foreword** and **Introduction** sections are important. They contain vital definitions and perspective that frames the message of Dream to Destiny. If you skipped them or haven't read them yet, I encourage you to go back and do so now.

You can live your dreams with passion and purpose. There is one *very* essential ingredient, though. You must *believe*. Believe without a hint of *doubt*. All things are possible for those who believe![10] But if you *don't* believe it, you will never achieve it. Whether you think you can or think you can't, *you're right!* Belief builds dreams, doubt kills them. Decide to believe in yourself and know that whatever your heart desires **is possible**. Your dreams can become reality if you believe.

Belief builds dreams. Doubt kills them.

Higher Power = God

In order for this program to work, it is vital that you recognize the existence of a Higher Power much greater than yourself. Make no mistake, my Higher Power is Almighty God — the One and Only. If you struggle with your belief in God or don't feel you understand the nature or presence of God, I encourage you to *stick with this book and the Dream Program!* It will still work for you and may help bring you to a place of spiritual clarity.

From my perspective, however, don't ask "the universe" to deliver what you want — it is a vast expanse of mostly empty space! Ask the One who *created* the universe. This way you'll tap into the Highest Power there is. You can do all things through the power of the Creator, God.[11]

Identify the source of power that is above and beyond you. I encourage you to think of this source as God, but you must make that choice for yourself.

As the popular song states, *"There will be miracles, when you believe..."*[12] Your prayers will be answered when you believe!

Getting Started

The DreamTouch Questionnaire (DTQ) exercise will get you in touch with your *true* dreams, passions, gifts and talents — your "natural resources" — and encourage you to believe in what's possible again. Please do the exercise exactly as instructed. Answer the questionnaire while having the included Atmosphere "Escape" DVD (aka, the "Focus DVD") playing in the background. (The Focus DVD comes with the Dream Program Kit.) You will need about 45 minutes of <u>quiet</u>, <u>uninterrupted</u> time to work through the DTQ. You must be alert, well rested, and in a good state of mind. *(Please do not attempt to go through the questionnaire if you are stressed, angry, in a hurry or distracted.)*

If you *do* all that is recommended for you in this method, miracles will happen in your life. Are you ready? Let's get started...

[Please proceed to the DreamTouch Questionnaire in Appendix A]

Practical: Follow the directions carefully. Complete the DTQ now.

Remember: If you want personal mentoring, coaching or guidance through any of the exercises that are part of the Dream Program visit www.DreamProgram.com/store.

Chapter 3

Your Gifts & Talents

"Hide not your talents. They for use were made. What's a sundial in the shade?" — Benjamin Franklin

Each of us has a unique set of gifts and talents. Your gifts and talents have been placed within you by Infinite Intelligence, and are as unique to you as your fingerprints. They are "natural resources" planted in you by design, with purpose and intent. Your gifts are meant to be used, exercised, strengthened and perfected! We are responsible to use what we've been given and to make the most of them. When we cultivate these natural resources, we reap a bountiful harvest.

One of the great ironies of our culture and educational system is that so much emphasis is placed on us getting better at the things we do poorly, rather than strengthening and getting even better at things we do well! Think about it. What we're gifted at usually comes quite naturally and easily for us. We develop skills quickly when we have innate talent. Yet, instead of being praised for what we do well, the focus all-too-often becomes what we do poorly or need improvement in. This is quite backwards, and something we need to adjust in our thinking. For instance, on a child's report card — do you focus on the A or the C? I admit, I've gravitated toward focusing on the negative in the past, but that has changed. As parents, we can look for these signs with our children and work to draw out their strengths rather than focus on their weaknesses.

Our gifts and talents are powerful indicators of the direction our lives should take. It is foolish for someone who is not gifted musically to pursue a musical career, no matter how much they love music. On the other hand, it is both irresponsible and wasteful for us not to use the gifts we have. If we are lazy and simply don't choose to exercise the gifts and talents we've been given, they will fade and eventually disappear. If you don't use them, you will lose them. However, if we exercise our gifts we will grow stronger in them, developing great skill and excellence. Not only that, but we are likely to discover other gifts and talents, increasing our value, contribution and impact on the world around us. [13]

Gifts vs. Talents

There are differences between "gifts" and "talents." Here's a closer look:

Gift — 1. Something given voluntarily without payment in return, so as to show favor or honor toward someone or make a gesture of assistance; a present. 2. Something bestowed or acquired without any particular effort by the recipient or without being earned. 3. A special ability or capacity; a natural endowment. 4. To present with as a gift; bestow gifts upon; to endow with.

Talent — 1. A special natural ability or aptitude. 2. A capacity for achievement or success; ability. 3. A talented person. 4. A group of persons with special ability. 5. Movies and Television. Professional actors collectively, esp. star performers. 6. A power of mind or body considered as given to a person for use and improvement. 7. Inclination or disposition.[14]

These, of course are definitions. Put simply, a "gift" is something freely given. It is not earned, it is bestowed — in our context here, it is bestowed upon us by God. On the other hand, a "talent" is a built in ability or potential. Similarly, it is placed within us by The Almighty, but it must be developed. They are closely related, but different. We all have both gifts and talents.

Focus on what you have, not on what you lack.
Use what you have to the fullest.

Most of my life I've been discouraged about all the gifts and talents I wanted, but seemed to lack. I am not gifted in athletics, piano, guitar or dance. I was not creatively or artistically gifted like my mother, husband or children. I don't have a photographic memory like my husband or other extremely intelligent people I know. I loved being involved with drama in high school, but was told I was not a great actress — this devastated me! I did some modeling in high school, but I was told my facial features weren't sharp enough and that I didn't have the "girl next door look" great models needed. I desperately wished I had these attributes, but I apparently did not. This really discouraged me!

Use Your Tools

Thankfully though, I have learned to use the tools I've got instead of worrying about those I don't. I now embrace and utilize the gifts that I have with an attitude of responsibility toward others. Since I was two years old, my father and mother told me I had a bright, bubbly "sunshine personality." My parents and others close to me said I lit up a room when I walked in. Soon after we met, my husband Mark wrote a song for me called, "You Shine So Bright." A good friend of mine over the years, Mike Joe, gave me the nickname "Sunshine." The Bible calls this "the gift of encouragement." I have learned to accept and embrace this **gift** and use it to benefit my family, friends and community. Volunteering and serving in the area of my gifts and talents makes me feel very happy and fulfilled. Currently I serve as a greeter/traffic controller in the morning at my children's elementary school and as a volunteer for the Parent Teacher Organization (PTO). Recently I started serving again as a greeter/usher at my church. For years I fulfilled my dream of singing on stage using my gifts of encouragement by performing and singing in the church choir and quartet. My husband and I exercise our gifts by conducting Dream Workshops to inspire people from all walks of life.

Additionally, I have a very hard work ethic, am very diligent and very driven. When I feel passionately about something, I go after it with focus and determination. Thankfully I have a strong business mind and am a natural entrepreneur. These are some of my other gifts.

My talents, on the other hand, are a bit different from my God-given gifts, yet they are related. In college, I chose to study business marketing, sales and communications. Additionally I received on the job sales training while in college with Kirby Vacuum selling vacuum cleaners door-to-door. After graduating, I received three years of intensive sales training with two Fortune 500 technology companies. As a result of all this training, I became a highly skilled, top sales producer for each of these companies.

These skills and talents coupled with my natural gifts were a strong combination when I started and ran my own technology company for more than eight years. Early in my career with these Fortune 500 companies, I saw inefficiencies and better ways to achieve results. I began to dream of having my own company and being independent. I began to visualize, focus and pray for this. Amazingly, within *one month* a door of opportunity opened when a former business associate called and described a new business model in our industry. It was a *perfect* fit for what I'd been visualizing. It was exactly the type of opportunity I was looking for! My dream manifested quickly! After visualizing, focusing and praying for what I wanted, God brought it to pass.

I started my business using a credit card with a $2,000 limit. I had a clear vision in my mind and a dream in my heart. With the talents and skills I had developed along with my natural gifts, I was able to replace my Fortune 500 corporate income within six months. As my business grew, I hired the right people to join my team. Within three years my income grew to more than four-times what it had been before. With all these ingredients, success with my first company came rather easily for me. It was fun and not that difficult because I tapped into the Power of God along with my gifts and talents to achieve these results.

Not My True Dream

Even though my company was successful and profitable, it was not my True Dream. After more than eight years I gave it up to pursue my TRUE Dreams and Passions, which I am doing now.

What are your gifts and talents? What comes so naturally and easily to you that you may even take it for granted, thinking that everyone has this gift? The DTQ™ will help you identify many of your unique gifts and talents. Some people are gifted communicators, while others are natural entrepreneurs. Some people are great empathizers, or gifted with encouragement, others excel at tough-minded disciplines such as athletics, martial arts, extreme fitness or specialized military service. Some are talented with making money, others at charitable efforts or community service. The list is long. These are but a few examples (Appendix C contains a Gift List you may find useful).

> *We each have different gifts, according to the grace given us... to each one the manifestation of the Spirit is given for the common good.*[15]

Are you using your gifts? We are intended to put our gifts and talents to work in order to benefit our families, our communities and "the common good." In this way we become the people we were intended to be. It is normal, in fact necessary for each of us to do this. When we pursue our healthy dreams and desires by way of our passions and gifts it becomes inevitable that we will achieve success and fulfillment. This brings great joy into our lives. Nothing is more natural.

We are meant to use all of our natural resources — our mind, our strength, our passions, our dreams, our gifts, our talents and our time — in order to become the people we are destined to be. This is the *only* way we will "step into our destiny." It is irresponsible not to do so!

> *Become who you're meant to be — step into your destiny.*

A "gift" is something we have been freely given. If we are not wise stewards of what we're given, it may be taken from us — our health, our wealth, our families, our friends, our gifts, our dreams, even our own life.[16]

We should also use our gifts and talents to build up the people around us — our families, our communities, our schools, our

38

businesses and professions. Whatever our gifts, we can contribute to the greater good through both self-benefit (i.e., "success") and the benefit of society at large, making a difference in the world around us. Bill Menghini was a great example of that...

William "Bill" Menghini did not finish high school, but at age 22 he started his first company. That company was called SASCO, an auto-parts supplier and distributor in the upper Midwest. It was the early 1920's and he saw great growth and opportunity in the auto industry. Later, William also founded and ran Pronto Auto Parts, Menco and Menghini & Co.

Because he was very passionate about helping people, Bill started and ran a newspaper that told the public the actual *truth*, instead of a sensationalized version of it. This newspaper never made any money, he ran it out of pure passion to make a difference and give people the straight story about matters and events.

He married his sweet heart, a smart college graduate, who became the wind beneath his wings. Together they used their natural resources — gifts, talents, time and passions — to build several successful companies that are still thriving to this day. William brought out the best in others, and was gifted in many ways. He was incredible with people, was very funny, a very hard worker, a positive thinker, compassionate, extremely generous, self-motivated and a visionary leader. He was passionate about the auto industry. He was passionate about helping people.

He owned a chain of auto parts stores across Illinois that employed hundreds of people for more than 40 years. With the profits he bought income producing real estate. A very smart investor, Bill bought an entire city block of commercial office buildings in Springfield, Illinois during The Great Depression. Later, he successfully developed real estate in Illinois, Florida and Arizona. Through these ventures he accumulated great wealth. They owned homes in Illinois, Florida and Arizona (to escape the Midwest winters) and traveled the world.

Bill was extremely generous. He *gave* SASCO to the employees 35 years after it was started. The Menghini's gave generously to several charities they were passionate about. Bill constantly served on community and association boards, volunteering his time. He was known for being impeccably honest. He used his gifts and passions to build these businesses, their community and the common good. Bill was a living example of the law of sowing and reaping. He sowed generous seeds into his businesses and the community, and reaped abundant rewards.

William Menghini was my grandfather — "Granddad" is what we called him. His dream was to build successful companies, create jobs and benefit the community. More than 20 years after his death, his impact is still being felt and he is still making a difference in the lives of many. His estate still receives trademark royalties, produces income, supports the needs of his daughter and gives to his grandchildren. He was a terrific example of a visionary leader who turned dreams into reality and benefited the common good.

Bill Menghini's goal was never to amass great wealth. He followed his passions, had a heart to help people and the community, and pursued opportunity with action and energy. He bubbled with enthusiasm, joy and a genuine love for people. He always believed that he could do anything! These attitudes and actions rewarded him with wealth, but wealth was not his goal.

Wealth

If your goal is wealth for wealth's sake, you are unlikely to achieve it. There has to be more behind it than that. You have to ask yourself a question — "Why do I want that?" If the answer is selfishly based, then your goal is shallow and self-serving. You may eventually achieve it, but only at great cost to you personally and in your lifetime.

My approach to the concept of wealth is similar to how I define success.[17] Wealth in my view is not measured by material possessions or financial net worth. Quality of life, character, fulfillment, joy, peace, quality relationships and a sense of purpose are the measures of wealth to me. We all have financial needs too, of course, and abundance is far better than lack. My deep conviction is that if you serve others in the area of your gifts, talents and passions, you will never be without.

I can't think of anyone who wouldn't like a million dollars to drop out of the sky and fall on their lap. I wouldn't mind that. You probably wouldn't either. But it's not going to happen. You may, on the other hand, get a million dollar idea! If you take action on it and pursue it with passion and purpose, then it may eventually produce wealth for you. But at that point, seeing your vision materialize, seeing the benefit it brings to others and the lives it changes will be the greater satisfaction. Any wealth experienced is a bonus!

There's nothing wrong with wealth or being wealthy. Financial success is almost always the fruit of hard work and much invested effort. However, if we pursue wealth as an ultimate achievement, we will be disappointed to find that when we get there it still feels empty unless there's something more meaningful behind it. The pursuit of riches, where our primary focus is material wealth is a modern-day form of idolatry where money can be a "god" that we worship. This "love of money" is the potential evil root we are warned about in Scripture.[18]

Israel's King Solomon, probably the richest man who ever existed, had this to say about the pursuit of wealth:

> Whoever loves money never has money enough; whoever loves wealth is never satisfied with his income... As goods increase, so do those who consume them. What benefit are they to the owner except to feast his eyes on them?[19]

Solomon declared that wealth and its pursuit was "meaningless, a chasing after the wind." We may achieve it, only to realize that the fulfillment it brings is very short-lived. Shortly after we ask, "Is that all there is?" On we go, chasing more conquest, greater achievements, more possessions, greater adventure, excitement, thrills or danger. It is a never-ending chase. With each new level we think, "Maybe *this* is the one which will satisfy..." only to be left feeling the void once again. Sure, it may be fun, temporarily exhilarating, and enjoyable for the moment, but it doesn't fill the void at the center of our soul. It *never* will. That's why Solomon called it "a chasing after the wind." You can't catch the wind.

The Rolls Royce

I know a very successful man who has been at the tip-top of his profession for a long time. He was one of my role models in the professional and business world. He was famous, highly sought after, richly compensated for his appearances and opinions, plus very wealthy. He invited me to lunch one day. This was a very rare privilege. He picked me up in his Rolls Royce. As I stepped in, I remarked, "Wow, what a beautiful car!" It was. He said, "It was always a dream of mine to own a Rolls Royce. So when I reached a certain goal, I rewarded myself with one. It is a beautiful car. But you know," he said, "it's needed quite a few repairs since I got it. It doesn't run very well sometimes, and I finally realized that it's just a car, like any other." I sensed a hint of melancholy in his voice as he said it. As we talked over lunch, I asked him many questions about his journey to the top and his life. It became quite clear to me that although he was successful, his business was squarely built around *him*. He had to be there, he had to run it and he had to star in it. He made a great deal of money when he did, but if he didn't work, his income stopped. He also shared with me some of the tolls success had taken on his personal life. As we talked, I knew he was sharing these things with me to help me gain perspective. I have never forgotten that discussion.

I'm sure you can think of examples where people of great wealth had disastrous personal or family lives. In the end, no amount of money or possessions will ever be enough to compensate for personal or family loss. At such points, wealth is truly "meaningless." Most would trade it all to have back what they just lost. Don't let this happen to you.

We also see great evidence that wealth in the hands of the young is not beneficial to them. Nowhere is this more visible than with "celebrities" in our culture — sports stars, heiresses, musicians and show business icons. If you put millions of dollars in the hands of an 18-25 year old, good things rarely happen. Most often, the tendency is towards excess and self-destructive behaviors. Only those smart enough, lucky enough or humble enough to have mentors, managers or coaches to guide them through the turbulence of paparazzi life escape trouble.

I Am My Best Me

You have been given natural resources from Infinite Intelligence — gifts and talents, dreams and passions. They take many forms. They are there by design. They are there for a reason. Are you being a great steward of what you've been given? Or are you being lazy, not even realizing or utilizing what you have?

In order to reach your intended destiny you must strive to do your very *best* with what you've been given — your natural resources. You should be your *best YOU!* Put your *best* foot forward in this life. Decide to be your best, do your best and look your best in everything you put your hand or mind to!

Be your Best. Do your Best. Look your Best.

Is it important to look your best? Yes! This means diet, exercise, rest and general hygiene. Most of us naturally realize these things. When we experience the benefits of actually doing them, we understand it even more. Besides, when we do these positive things we feel better, think better, have better attitudes, make better decisions and experience far better overall results in our lives.

Many have given up on themselves either personally or professionally — appearance, weight, clothing, hygiene or health. Don't let this happen! Those who go this route have lost vision and are choosing to give up on life! *Where there is no vision, people cast off restraint.*[20] Put another way, where there is no vision, people perish. They start to die physically, spiritually, mentally, emotionally

42

and financially. It is never too late to improve in any area of life, but the longer you wait the tougher the road to improvement becomes. Please don't give up and don't let this happen. If we do, we are choosing to allow ourselves to *perish.*

I am my Best Me!

"I am my Best Me" is a phrase that I say to myself often and teach to my children. "All I can do is my best" is another phrase that I say to myself because all that we can be and do is our best. If we are not doing our best, we know it internally. If we're slacking at something, just getting by or skating by doing the minimum, our inner voice speaks to us saying, "You know you could do *much* better than that. Why don't you give it your best and show them how good you really are?" Deep down inside, we know we've held something back or not taken our best shot. This creates an inner disharmony that troubles us. Instead, when we've taken our best shot, given something all we have — even if we come up short — we're at peace, because we know that we did our best. This leaves no lingering regret. Do yourself a favor — and those you are partnered with or work for — a favor and "be your best you." You'll be glad you did.

Choosing Your Path

Few people choose their life professions based on their dreams and passions or gifts and talents. Most people choose their careers based on the income potential, their college degree or something that coincides with their children's school schedule. Even if you have been in your vocation for many years you can change and go in the direction of your dreams. You might have to scale down your life style, but isn't it worth it to achieve happiness and peace? Consider the inspiring story of Jason Beskind, who made just such a decision…

Jason Beskind was a high-powered attorney for over 12 years making over $250,000 per year owning his own law firm. He often worked 12+ hour days. Stress was affecting him so much that he was having frequent migraines and experiencing other health issues. He was young, only in his mid 30's. His real passion and gift was cooking. His *true dream* was to be a chef in his own restaurant.

He decided to pursue his dream, closed his law firm and bought a restaurant franchise. Jason and his family sold their $1.5 million dollar home along with their expensive furniture and nice cars. They started their life over on the solid foundation of their dreams, passions and gifts. Their family is much more unified now and full of joy. Their new restaurant is doing fantastically well despite the current recession because its leader has a supernatural gift, energy and passion for what he's doing.[21]

Cultivate the natural gifts and talents of your children, helping them hone and perfect their strengths, instead of focusing on their weaknesses. The Jewish culture has been doing this consistently for thousands of years and there is a well-known history of success because of this. Here are a few secrets to training children that have been passed down through generations in the Hebrew culture. It should be no surprise that these secrets come directly from the Scriptures. Perry Stone gives an excellent synopsis of this in his book, _Breaking the Jewish Code_:

Jewish Secrets to Training Children for Success

From a Hebraic perspective, training a child is more than consistently instructing a child in right and wrong. Every child is born with a distinct personality, certain inner gifts and abilities that are as unique as that child's individual fingerprints. As children grow from infant to child, child to teen, and teen to young adult, the parents are to discern the inclinations and possible gifts within the child's personality, tapping into the possibilities of how **God can and will use the child to fulfill his or her appointed destiny**. Scripture tells us: "**Delight yourself in the Lord** and **he will give you** the desires of your heart" (Psalm 37:4). Traditionally, this has been interpreted as, "Whatever we desire God will give it to us." We know God answers prayer and grants petitions (John 14:13; 16:23). However, another way of interpreting Psalm 37:4 is that **God gives or places in our hearts**, certain desires that **He will help us** to fulfill. Christian teenagers often request prayer for God's will to be done in their lives. I reply, "What do you feel deep in your spirit that you want to do? After they answer the question, I respond, "Then make preparations to do it." Their concern is, "What if it is not what God wants?" The answer is, "Who do you think gave you that desire in your heart and the inclination toward that particular gift or career? **God gave you those desires and God will help you fulfill them**." These inclinations begin early in life and directing them must begin early.[22] (Emphasis mine)

Joshua Bell, the world famous violinist, went from Dream to Destiny using his gifts and passions. When Joshua was three years old his parents noticed him plucking tunes with rubber bands he had stretched around the handles of his dresser drawers. At age four, Joshua's parents bought him his first violin. By age 12 he had become very serious about the instrument, thanks in large part to the inspiration of renowned violinist Josef Gingold, who became his beloved teacher and mentor.

Joshua Bell came to national attention at the age of 14 in a highly acclaimed orchestral debut. Mr. Bell received an Artist Diploma in Violin Performance from Indiana University. He has been named an "Indiana Living Legend" and received the Indiana Governor's Arts Award. For more than two decades, Joshua Bell has enchanted audiences worldwide with his breathtaking virtuosity and tone of rare beauty.

He is a Grammy Award winning violinist and has been inducted into the Hollywood Bowl Hall of Fame. He has played to crowds in every major concert hall in America, at the White House and was staged as a street musician in the Washington D.C. metro station in a now famous video that was done as a sketch for The Tonight Show in 2009. With more than 30 CD recordings, Mr. Bell's newest album, "At Home with Friends," was number one on Classical and Crossover Charts in October 2009. Joshua chose to pursue a career as a classical violinist because it was his dream, his passion, his gift and his LOVE.

Stephen Key, co-founder of **InventRight**, is another terrific example of someone who uses his gifts and talents to achieve his dreams. Stephen pursued and achieved his dream of becoming a successful, self-supporting inventor. He has used his gift for innovation to create many new products over the past 20+ years as his full time profession. With millions of dollars in royalties from his many inventions, he's able to live the life of his dreams in Northern California. Stephen has built his business around his family and friends so that he can spend quality and quantity time with them. He loves his work and truly enjoys helping other inventors achieve their dreams as well. Learn more about Stephen's work at **www.InventRight.com.**

Stephen came highly recommended to me from several credible sources, so I hired Stephen as my mentor for our invention business. A few months later (as mentioned before) he encouraged me to apply for the ABC Reality TV Show "Wife Swap" because he knew they were looking for mom inventors. Our episode features a few pieces of our patent pending method. Stephen also referred *The Los Angeles Times* to me for an interview about two of our patent pending products, which they voted in the top 3 out of 9 innovations created during the 2009 recession. What incredible publicity, thanks to Stephen.

You are no different than Joshua or Stephen. They simply discovered their gifts and passions, had the courage to accept their dreams as real possibilities and went after them. Their success was inevitable because they were tapping into their natural resources. Sure, they had to work at it, apply themselves and put their best efforts forward, but so can you. Infinite Intelligence gave you unique gifts and passions for a reason. Your responsibility is to *USE* them for the common good. You'll find joy, peace and your Divine Destiny if you follow this path.

Your Best Foot Forward

Strive to be your best, do your best and look your best — be your best *you*! Take care of what the Infinite One has entrusted you with. Put it to work. When you make the effort to look your best for your spouse and children, you are giving them a good example to follow. On the other hand if you let yourself go, eating whatever you want whenever you want it, not exercising or taking care of yourself, you are not respecting yourself or your body. Not only are you setting a poor example for your children or spouse, it's likely to have other implications in your intimacy and relationships in general.[23]

I am amazed and very pleased that my first grade son comes home with materials that teach these principles from his public school. In his first week of first grade, he came home with an agreement from his teacher that asked him to commit to making his best efforts and do his best work during the year. He was expected to read it and sign it — like a contract! If these principles are good for our elementary school-aged children, they're good for us too!

Put your best foot forward in life utilizing all of your natural resources and doors will open for you everywhere you go. Encourage those around you to utilize their gifts and talents to pursue their dreams and passions. Start with your children, family, friends and others close to you. You can change things in your own life and affect your destiny beginning right NOW!

Practical: Using your journal or notebook, make an exhaustive list of your gifts and talents. If it is helpful to you, refer to the Gift List in Appendix C. Remember, the list in Appendix C is only a partial list of Gifts you may possess, there are many others. Distinguish between Gifts and Talents based on the definitions provided earlier in this chapter. Use two columns — one for "Gifts" the other for "Talents." You may also want to refer to the DTQ for valuable input it may provide. Take your time. Brainstorm here.

It is also helpful to get outside input from friends or family who know you well, since we do not normally see ourselves objectively. For this or other exercises, be careful to choose *only* people who are positive and encouraging to provide input or give you feedback.

Reality TV Bite: The other family in our Wife Swap episode had very different values and priorities than we do. This was no surprise because they purposely choose complete opposites. My husband and I believe they had given up on many areas of their life — health, diet, nutrition, exercise, hygiene and weight — their own personal excellence. And they certainly weren't using their God-given gifts. Of course, they're free to make these choices, but we were sad to see the toll it had taken on the parents. I was particularly concerned about the impact this would have on their children's future. My husband shared the very verse of Scripture (Proverbs 29:18) noted above with the "swap" mom while she was at our home. We both felt they had "*cast off restraint.*" They certainly weren't striving to be their best, and it showed. It was also preventing them from turning their economic situation around. Enjoying spontaneous fun and living for the moment is fine, but when your health threatens your very life, and you're on the verge of homelessness because of your decisions, you've got to take a hard look at yourself and make some changes! Consider being "my Best Me" and using your gifts and talents to turn your life around. It starts with a simple decision. This was a central part of the message we shared with them.

Remember: If you need personal mentoring, coaching or guidance through any of the exercises that are part of the Dream Program visit www.DreamProgram.com/store.

Chapter 4

Getting in Good with The Boss

The eyes of the LORD range throughout the earth to strengthen those whose hearts are fully committed to him.[24]

It's always good to have a great relationship with your boss. It usually makes things much better at work. God is the ultimate boss. As the Creator and Omnipotent Ruler, he is both the ultimate authority and Omnipresent Power over all things. The good news is that he wants to be your Best Friend. He's the perfect parent who loves you so thoroughly and completely (more than a human parent is capable of loving their child) it is actually beyond our ability to understand.

What God seeks from you is a relationship. He wants to walk alongside you in your life. He desires closeness with you that is warm and intimate. He wants to hear how you feel — good, bad or ugly — throughout each day. Even though he knows all things, he still wants to hear from you, because he loves you and created you to be in a loving relationship with him.

God wants to bless you with good things — abundance, relationships, peace, fulfillment, joy and more. He wants you to prosper and have a life full of good things. He wants you to remain free from harm.[25] He has great plans for your life, for it to be full of **good** things. What parent doesn't want good things for their children?[26] How much more does the Father want them for us?

To be sure, God is not a "candy store" keeper who's going to give us whatever we want. Any responsible parent wouldn't give their kids anything they wanted, knowing that some things aren't good for them. The Father will always keep our best interest in mind. In his infinite wisdom and foresight, he sees down the road to the bigger picture. Sometimes he has to protect us from ourselves. We, in turn, have to escape the self-centered mindset of two-year-olds and gain a mature perspective about the difference between our "wants" and our true "needs."

Walk in Submission

The word "submission" is one we struggle with so much, especially in America. We bristle at the thought because we don't like to be submissive to *anyone!* Yet we have to submit to our bosses, our teachers, coaches or supervisors every day. The idea shouldn't be so foreign to us.

It is wise to learn to walk in submission and obedience to God. He wants this for our good. He has given us his Word to direct us in his wisdom and his will for our lives. When we seek to please him, it endears us to him even more. That is not to say that if you obey God, you'll get what you want — God cannot be manipulated. He knows the motives of your heart (and mind). However, when you have a child-like heart[27] and attitude toward your Creator, confiding in him as you would your best friend, he is pleased to show you favor. Try it! What do you have to lose? Make the Lord of heaven and earth your best friend. Be completely honest and open with him about what's on your heart and mind. Seek him with all your heart and you will find him.[28] This will warm his heart and encourage him to reveal himself to you more and more.

Think back in your life to the time that you best connected with the Lord. Was it through journaling, praying on your knees, watching a beautiful oceanfront sunset or hiking to a mountaintop? Do now whatever you did before that was successful in connecting with the Lord. Make it your goal to connect with him again every day.

The LORD is good to all; he has compassion on all he has made.[29]

Perhaps you don't realize how much he truly loves you. Maybe you struggle with your belief in God or you've never experienced a connection with him. If you have not connected with him before, try the things mentioned above. For many, journaling is a great way to connect with him. Write him a letter in your journal. Tell him what you're grateful for. He loves it when his kids are grateful, just like we love it when our kids are grateful. He wants to shower you with more to be grateful for. Isn't this how we are with our own children? So it is with the Father!

On the flip side, what if your child is ungrateful and complaining about what they have? As a parent, you might say, "If you're not grateful for this, I may have to take it away and help you get some perspective." God disciplines us as a father disciplines his child[30] — out of love — to teach us important life lessons that help us grow in the long run. Now turn that example inward. Ask yourself, "What about me? Am I grateful?" Perhaps you need to get some perspective.

From Shepherd Boy to King

I share these great secrets with you to help you connect in your relationship with the Infinite One. King David was a great example. As a young shepherd boy, often alone in the pasture, he made God his best friend. He talked with God as he tended the sheep. He wrote songs to God and sang to him often. He relied on the

Almighty when he overpowered the bear, the lion and later the giant, Goliath.

God said about David that this young shepherd boy was a "man after his own heart." This is why he was anointed by God to be king. David wrote much of the book of Psalms. They were poems, prayers and songs to the Father — a lot like *journaling!* This practice made David's relationship with the LORD legendary. These events were recorded so that we could learn from them and apply these examples to our own lives.

> "The LORD has sought out a man after his own heart and
> appointed him leader..."[31]

I want to imitate David's heart in my walk with God. How would you like the Father to say that you had a heart after his own heart? If you seek him and strive to please him, there's no reason he wouldn't. You and I can have this same kind of relationship — it is within our reach. He wants each of us to love him with all of our heart, soul, mind and strength.[32] Go for it and see what happens in your life!

Talk to God like he's your best friend. Why? Because he wants to know your true heart and be your closest relationship. He wants an intimate friendship with you and he cares for you.[33] He wants you to trust and rely on him. He promises to provide for you and take care of you. He wants to be your best friend forever — your "BFF" as my daughter likes to say!

Take Problems Upstairs

It's much better to share your true feelings and thoughts — good, bad and ugly — with God rather than with your spouse or friends, because he can actually do something about each situation. This is not to say that we shouldn't talk to those closest to us (spouse, friends or family) about problems or life's challenges. Certainly we need people in our lives that we can be completely honest and open with. However, your spouse or friends don't have the power to change people's hearts. God does.[34] Taking your problems "upstairs" is often the best solution.

When you pray or talk to the Creator about problems or challenges, you are being solution oriented. On the other hand, if you talk to your spouse about how upset you are at your friend, how do you think your spouse will view your friend in the future? It is bound to taint your spouse's view of your friend. When we share how we're feeling about another person who is absent, this may actually become gossip, or even worse, slander. In the same way, if you talk with your parents about how upset you are with your spouse, how do you think your parents will view your spouse in the future? You get the point.

It is not healthy in any way to gossip or slander.[35] It never accomplishes anything good. It only causes harm. Therefore, talk to God about how you feel when people hurt you. Ask God for wisdom and guidance on how to work it out between the two of you. Seek out answers in his Word. He will provide the guidance and assistance you need. Then go directly to that person and work it out in a solution-oriented way, settling matters quickly.[36]

Seek and Ask

Over the past 24 years, God has given me most of what I've asked for. I truly believe that He saw a pure, child-like heart and wanted to bless me, showering his divine favor upon me. He wants to do the same for you. Seek a relationship with him. Seek to please him out of a pure heart and see what he does. Test him in this.[37] He invites us to ask, so we shouldn't be afraid to. He'll give you **more** than you ask for or imagine.[38] It's all about walking in a relationship with him, loving him and pleasing him by doing what's right in his eyes — which means obeying his Word (The Bible).[39]

The natural question is "What about when God *doesn't* answer my prayers? What about when his answer is 'no'?" I believe that if you are connected in relationship with him, his Spirit guides your heart and mind. To be sure, many times the answer may be "no" to our requests or desires. Not all of our requests or desires are good or healthy, nor would all of them be good for us if we got them. Here's what happens though; when we are connected with the Almighty in relationship, his Spirit guides us. When we are conversing with God in prayer and in his Word, he will guide us in the way we should go. He guides us in different directions, often in a better way than what we had in mind to begin with. He will plant or inspire new ideas and aspirations in us. He will change what we think, what we want and which direction we go. He will open new doors for us. He will change *our* heart! What God changes is *You!* All things will work toward a new and greater good.[40]

My massage therapist, Melody, shared her story with me recently. She told me that God was absolutely her *best friend!* She told me she talks to God about *everything*. She also said she asks him for what she needs. She said, "You know, when I ask, he gives me what I need *every time!*" It was so sweet. You can tell by talking to her that she has a very warm and intimate relationship with her Heavenly Father. Examples like Melody encourage and inspire me.

God wants a great and close relationship with you. He loves you more than you could possibly imagine! He wants to bless you with good things. So let go and give him your heart. Delight yourself in the Lord and he will give you the desires of your heart.[41] To delight yourself in the Lord means to find your delight, your happiness and joy in him.

Jesus encourages us to ask, seek and knock on the door of what we desire and hope for. We are encouraged to ask, and it will be given to us; seek and we will find what we're looking for; knock and the door will be opened for us. Isn't this encouraging? On the other hand, if we *don't* ask, it *won't* be opened for us. God is your Heavenly Father who loves you and wants to give you good things. What parent doesn't want to give good things to their children? How much more does the Father of all creation, want to give good things to his children who ask?[42]

Get to know God's heart for you. Read and enjoy his Word. Make him your best friend. You won't regret it. Who knows what he may have in mind for you? You have everything to gain and nothing to lose. Get in good with the Boss.

Practical: Have a conversation with God like you would your best friend. Find a solitary place and just have a friendly, open conversation with him. Don't worry about keeping it short, go as long as you'd like — God has time for you. If this doesn't work for you, write him a letter in your journal. If you like, pray or talk through it with him after you've finished.

If you struggle with your belief in God, try a conversation with him. Ask him in some unique or personal way to show you his presence in your life. You may be surprised by what happens.

Reality TV Bite: One central part of our family's life that was not captured at all during our "Wife Swap" episode was our spiritual life. We are passionate about our relationship with God, his Word and helping others in their walk with him. The show's producers chose not to include any aspect of this part of our lives at all, either with my husband and I personally, with our children, or the many we are connected with in close relationships. It would have been our preference to acknowledge God's presence and the many amazing miracles he's done in our lives, giving him full credit and glory for the success and victories we've achieved.

Chapter 5

Words

Pleasant words are like honeycomb, sweet to the soul and healing for the bones.[43]

Your thoughts are extremely important to both your wellbeing and the outcomes of your life. Equally important to your thoughts are your *Words*. These are both the words you speak to others and those spoken to yourself in the mind (self-talk).

Words have power, just as our thoughts have power. They have the power to build up and the power to destroy. Positive words have the power to heal us mentally and physically. As we take control of the thoughts we allow ourselves to think, and the words we allow ourselves to speak, we will be promoting not only our own health, but also the health of those around us.

The tongue has the power of life and death.[44]

The destructive power of words is also enormous. A terrible fire can be started with the spark of just one negative word. The tongue also can set the whole course of a person's life on fire.[45] Have you ever noticed this in your own life? I have. When I've slipped and said something hurtful to my husband, for example, because of a grudge in my heart, our relationship took a hit. Even though I told him how sorry I was for what I said and he forgave me, there was still a consequence. We cannot take back our words. If we don't keep a tight rein on our tongues, our religion is worthless.[46]

How many of us have had someone in our life that tore us down with what they said to us? Do you know parents who say damaging words to their children, stepchildren or children-in-law? I've seen the profound affect that parents' words, positive or negative, have on their children. Horrible statements like, "You'll never amount to anything" and "You're a loser" or worse have driven teenagers to drug abuse and suicide. On the other hand, the parents who controlled their emotions and their words raised wonderful, emotionally stable children who would never even think of defiling their minds and bodies with drugs or suicidal tendencies.

Words can leave emotional scars for life that are very painful. Once said, the damage is done and cannot be taken back. My father said these and many other terrible things to me in my life. It still haunts me sometimes. I have had to battle vigorously to overcome the effects of this, but it can be done!

Drug Court Kids

Mark and I conduct workshops for at risk teens on probation in the Arizona state court system. For the most part they are minors who have been convicted of drug offenses. The majority of the troubled teenagers that we've met have at least one parent who does not have a tight rein on their tongue. This parent is often an alcoholic, a drug addict, mentally ill, a rageaholic, physically or verbally abusive and in the habit of saying hurtful words to their children like, "What's wrong with you? Are you deaf? Are you stupid? You're a slut. You're a whore. You're crazy. I wish you were dead," and the like. It should be no surprise that these teens turn to drugs and alcohol to mentally escape the recurring words that play over and over again in their minds like a broken record. Having their teens turn to drug abuse is only one of many consequences the parents face. Some young people end up in jail, as runaways living on the streets or dead because of their parents' verbal abuse.

Our objective is to teach the kids and the parents how to retrain their minds (both conscious and subconscious) using this The 7 Key method. It is so rewarding to see entire families turn around after applying our process. When they learn to focus on their dreams they get a new sense of vision and purpose for their lives. *Where there is no vision people perish,* so it follows that people need vision to thrive and prosper.

When faced with negative, damaging words from one or both parents, you can break the chain and reverse the cycle. A young man named Steven who I am working with comes from such a background. He is handsome, talented and athletically gifted. Unfortunately, like so many, his father has rarely had a good word to say to him. All of Steven's life his father has told him he was worthless, was a loser and wouldn't amount to anything. Often this tendency has been passed down generationally. *His* father told *him* those things, and now he's repeating them to his own children. This is how sin is passed down from generation to generation. With God's help I am training Steven to break the chain, believe in himself and all that he's capable of. Within the next four years, Steven will be playing in the National Football League!

The Science of Words

Japanese scientist, Dr. Masaru Emoto, studied the effect that words have on water. The results of his study were alarming. Dr. Emoto attached various words and phrases to water bottles then tested the water's reaction after exposure to them. The words and phrases were both positive and negative. He then photographed the water crystals after freezing them using a high-powered microscope. The crystals formed in the water exposed to positive words and phrases were remarkable. Several examples are shown here. As you can see, "Love and Appreciation," "Thank You" and an "Offering of Prayer" caused beautifully shaped crystals to form. Similar patterns were observed with "Peace," blessings and other positive expressions.

Water Molecule,
Before Offering a Prayer

Water Molecule,
After Offering a Prayer

Thank You

You Make Me Sick,
I Will Kill You

Love and Appreciation

The water exposed to the phrases "You make me sick" and "I will kill you" caused the water to crystallize in deformed, irregular patterns.[47] If words can do this to water, imagine what words can do to us, considering that we are made up of 70 percent or more of water?

Growing up Mom told me, "You can have, do and be anything in your life that you want." "Your body is a temple of the Holy Spirit." "Ask and you shall receive." "I love you!" Thankfully mom built us up with these life giving, edifying words. Because I was a child, I believed all these statements and they became the foundation of my faith and relationship with the most perfect parent, my Heavenly Father. Mom gave her three girls the greatest gift of all, faith and a relationship with God. This is the most important relationship of all. With this small seed of faith, I was able through the power of the Almighty to turn my heart, mind and life around, breaking the curse of all the destructive, negative things I heard growing up. You can do the same.

We have a profound affect on the people around us. We must choose to be loving and treat others with kind words and actions. If we speak to one another in love, building others up according to their needs and for their benefit, we will improve the lives of those around us remarkably.[48] Remember, the whole reason we are here on earth is to use our gifts to build up those around us for "the common good." If we simply observe the Golden Rule — to treat others the way we want to be treated — we'll be a part of the solution instead of part of the problem.

Self-Talk

Perhaps even more influential than words spoken by others, are the words we speak to ourselves. Our "self-talk" is vitally important to our overall condition, both mentally and physically. Inner thoughts are self-talk. Sometimes we literally talk to ourselves, but most of the time our self-talk is in thought form.

How do you talk to yourself? What do you tell yourself? If you're like most people, the answers are not good. Most people are very self-condemning, express thoughts of failure and insecurity. That's the norm. Pretty sad, when our worst enemy is "us." This must change!

Whatever is excellent or praiseworthy, think about such things.[49]

As a matter of first importance, we simply must take control of our self-talk and tell ourselves positive, encouraging, constructive things. We must believe in ourselves and channel our thinking with confidence. I'm not talking about arrogance — it is inexcusable and never justified. I'm talking about believing in yourself and telling yourself positive things. It's bad enough when others speak negative or damaging words to us. There's absolutely no reason we should do that to ourselves, and yet most people do. This is the very first thing we need to turn around. Once we do, it's the beginning of turning our lives in the direction we want them to go.

My husband tells me that the greatest challenge for athletes at the highest level of any sport is the battle that goes on their minds. They must train themselves to *believe* that can do whatever it is – — making the shot, the play, getting the hit or whatever; then they learn to *visualize* themselves doing it successfully. This is exactly the process we're talking about.

"If you think you can or think you can't — you're right!" Henry Ford

It starts with belief. If you don't believe you can do something, then you won't be able to do it. If you believe you can, you will. It starts with your inner beliefs, thoughts and self-talk. We must commit to the habit of telling ourselves positive, encouraging, belief-building things, learning to eliminate the self-sabotage that is so natural for most of us. We have to be on *our* side!

Boundaries

Recently I decided to draw strong boundaries in my life. When friends or family members say hurtful words to me, my children or my husband we tell them that we do not tolerate negative talk or treatment. If they blow it, we'll give them one more chance. If it doesn't change, we will limit or eliminate our exposure to them. We forgive them, but at the same time, we won't continue to expose ourselves to harmful talk or treatment. We teach our children not play with people who are mean or can't play nice. We lead by example.

Why put ourselves around negative influences? If we don't stand up for what's right, we'll fall. I wish I would've learned this simple rule when I was a child. If I had, I would have avoided a great deal of heartache in my life. For many years I chose to stay in destructive relationships that tore me down. I didn't know any better because that was the relationship model I had growing up. I've learned that I don't have to be around people filled with negative words or behaviors.

Before we go to visit family in their homes or cities, we lay out this boundary for them. If they want us to come visit, all we ask is that they are pleasant and speak kind words. We tell them in advance that if they start talking negatively we'll have to leave and will not return until they can be pleasant. These family dynamics are sometimes the most destructive in our lives.

If someone we know is rude or mean on the telephone, we tell them calmly that we need to hang up now because we don't engage in malicious talk or negative discussions. We teach our children that if they can't say something nice, they should not say anything at all. We've conveyed this to our friends and family also. We are choosing to protect ourselves from the damaging effects of negative words. We encourage you to do the same. Decide what your boundaries are, set them and keep them.

The Golden Rule:
In everything, do to others what you would have them do to you, for this sums up the Law.[50]

Live by The Golden Rule. Choose to speak edifying words and they will come back to you. This is called "the boomerang effect" — whatever you do will come back to you. This might also be referred to as the Law of Sowing and Reaping. You will reap just what you sow; therefore treat others the way you want to be treated.

Two Powerful Words

The two most powerful words that you can say to yourself are, "I am." This is how the Almighty described himself — as the great I AM. His Spirit lives within us — heart, mind and soul. We are connected to him in Spirit. He breathes life into us daily (hoping and waiting for us to choose a relationship with him). He can take our breath and life away in an instant. When we make "I am…" statements centered on the dreams for our lives, we tap into the kingdom and power of the Almighty that is within us. Remember, the Kingdom of Heaven is *within us!* When we say "I am" we are cultivating his power within our hearts. This is a big part of how we manifest, not by our own power, but by the power of the Almighty.

Don't just accept who you are right now, weaknesses and all. Design your character around the person you want to become. You can change! Tap into the Spirit that lives in your heart by saying "I am…" based on who you wish to become. This is an ACTION of faith! When you do this you begin creating new realities for yourself based on values and priorities you establish. I do this daily and pray aloud through my "I am" statements.[51] After praying through them, I spend time meditating and visualizing my specific dreams. When my faith is exercised like this I am tapping into the power of the great I Am living in me to manifest the new realities I desire.

When I pray like this I am also re-programming my subconscious mind. My subconscious mind directs my conscious mind and therefore my life. Declaring these statements out loud with positive expectancy demonstrates confidence that God will bring them about. When I do this I am acting in faith that God will work in and through me according to his good purpose. I'm not asking him for anything outrageous. Why wouldn't he want to bless me in this way? God promises that we will abound in all good things and that all things are possible for those who believe. I choose to trust that he is faithful to his promises.

Another reason to say "I am" is to take responsibility for your own actions. We only have control over our own thoughts, words and actions. You cannot control your spouse, your children, or anyone else. When you say "I am" you are focusing on what *you* can do about things, and how *you* can change to become better. That's why I say, "I am my best me. I do my best in all things." In this way I take responsibility for my own life and my own actions. Join me and choose to lead by example.

The Key Cards™ are a very important step in this seven step method of manifesting dreams (the Key Card concept and instructions are discussed in detail in Appendix D). This exercise will train you to feed your mind positive, constructive, health-building words. Choose carefully worded statements on your Key Card, because they will manifest in your life. For example, instead of writing down "I am debt free" write, "I am financially free." Notice the difference? A focus on "debt" will bring you more of it because the subconscious mind manifests what you think and say. Instead of saying "I am never late" say "I am always prompt." Being financially free and prompt will become your new realities with persistent prayer, visualization and action. It is very important to construct positively worded statements for your Key Cards for use during your prayer/meditation times; further details provided in Appendix D.

When you pray out loud through your Key Cards daily, you'll be tapping into The 3 Powers™ (Mind, Passion and God) simultaneously and persistently. In the Parable of the Persistent Widow[52] the point Jesus makes is that God answers the persistent prayers of his people "quickly." My experience and deep conviction is that with persistent prayer, passionate focus and your subconscious mind, results will manifest *quickly* in your life.

The "Manifesting Instructions" (Appendix B) will instruct you to pray through your Key Cards just before falling asleep and immediately upon rising in the morning. Your mind is most relaxed during these times of day. What you feed your mind during these crucial times will sink deeply into your subconscious. This is also called your "deeper mind." I work to *feel* the feelings and emotions associated with my specific dreams or desires when I'm praying and visualizing.

Your deeper subconscious mind never sleeps. It works around the clock, either for you or against you. Instead of watching TV or the news just before bed, pray out loud through your Key Cards, visualize and feel yourself realizing your dreams. This puts your subconscious mind to work *for you* while you're sleeping, instead of against you. Your deeper mind is connected to the Infinite Mind (the mind of God) and will create ways to bring your dreams into reality.

Watching TV before bed may seem innocent, but is actually a very destructive habit. When you do this, you're filling your mind with the twisted images of modern-day media, and that's what fills your subconscious mind while you sleep. Instead, replace this with the great habit of praying through your Key Cards, expressing positive words, thoughts and feelings before sleep. You will be filling your mind with your highest priority dreams, passions and aspirations. It only takes 21 days — three weeks — to form a new habit. Forming this healthy new habit will change your life to be better than ever! Try it and you'll see.

Take our 30-day challenge. Pray through your Key Cards out loud every morning and night upon waking and falling asleep and see what happens in your life. Visualize your dreams and feel yourself achieving them. Control the direction of your mind by doing this simple exercise diligently for 30 days. You will be training your mind to become all that you ask or imagine and re-directing the course of your life. You'll re-train your words to be positive, constructive and healing. Journal what happens in your life. You may find that your relationships improve dramatically. You may see doors open for you in the direction of your dreams. You have nothing to lose by taking this simple 30-day challenge. Start today.

Examples of Dina's "I am" statements:

I am *my best, I do my best, I look my best,* I am *my Best ME!* I am *who I want my children to become.* I am *a strong & successful business woman earning over $X/year.* I am *an excellent steward of all I am blessed with.* I am *giving back generously plus saving for retirement & education.* I am *fit for life, 114 pounds, healthy and strong.*

Practical: Construct several "I am" statements based on your DTQ™, your gift assessment and some inner reflection. Some deep meditation and/or prayer time is recommended prior to this exercise. Write as many as you would like, applying to any and all areas of your life. Choose positive, constructive, proactive words for use in your statements, because this is what will manifest in your life.

Reality TV Bite: Right after I had the vision and desire to share our message of hope with the world, I verbally told my husband that we were going to share Dream to Destiny on national television one year ago. We had zero contacts in the TV industry. My husband said, "I know!" That very night I received the e-mail about the Reality TV show opportunity. I responded and the producer called the next day and interviewed me on the spot. Verbalize your visions and desires to a trusted, positive friend and see what happens. Experience the power of your words.

Remember: We're here for you if you would like personal mentoring, coaching or other guidance through these exercises or the Dream Program in general at www.DreamProgram.com/store.

Part II

The 3 Powers™

There are three great powers available to you, which can help you manifest your dreams into realities. The 3 Powers™ can give you the strength and ability to embrace your divine destiny, if you will utilize them.

These powers are:

The Power of the Mind

The Power of Passion

The Power of God

Chapter 6

The Power of the Mind

"Whatever the mind can conceive and believe it can achieve."
— Napoleon Hill

The mind is incredibly powerful. Our brain is intricately complex and sophisticated. It is an amazing creation. Even after decades of supercomputing advances and development, science is only able to produce a fraction of the processing capability and complexity of the human brain.[53]

The human mind sets us apart from all other creatures known to us. Our ability to reason, think, deduce and choose sets us apart from the rest of creation. Man alone is able to adjust himself to any reasonable climate or environment, free of the control of nature. Man alone has relational abilities above and beyond the animal kingdom. Man is the only "creature" that mates year round; all other "mating" is seasonal. Yes we have instincts, but we can ponder, analyze and choose unlike any other creature.

Perhaps the greatest ability we've been given is the power to choose. Our feelings and emotions are a product of our thoughts and choices. And yet this freedom of choice is probably the one we take most for granted. For instance, God does not *force* us to choose a relationship with him. He allows us to make that choice — or not. He wants us to. He hopes we will. But we are not made as robots programmed to obey his commands. It is up to us to decide. He has promised eternal benefits and rewards for choosing him, but it is completely up to us to make that decision. This freedom is very powerful!

Our intellect alone is an incredible gift. All thought, consciousness, awareness, reasoning and decision occur through the mind. Our mind is our very *being.* We have a physical body, but our *spirit,* our *essence,* or our *soul* exists through our mind. In fact, when Scripture refers to your "heart," it is really referring to your "mind."[54] Your heart is a pump, and an *amazing* one at that, but nothing more. Your mind is where all feeling, emotion, passion and desire reside — all of these are related to the "heart."

So when the creation account states that *God created man in his own image*[55] it is referring to spirit or mind. It does not mean we *look* like God, with arms, legs, eyes, a nose, etc. It means we *are* like him in Spirit and in Mind. God is Divine Mind, Universal Mind, Infinite Mind and Infinite Intelligence. Our minds are connected to the Mind of God. We sense his presence in our very essence.

Conscious vs. Subconscious Mind

Your mind functions on two different levels, the conscious and the subconscious.[56] Summarized simply, the conscious mind controls all voluntary, waking and intentional functions. The subconscious mind accounts for all involuntary, sleep-state and unconscious functions. Although absolute numbers cannot be proven, neuroscience experts estimate that approximately 10 percent of brain/mind function is accounted for by conscious activity and 90 percent by subconscious activity, including a large percentage that is mysterious, unexplained or underutilized. Involuntary actions such as breathing, swallowing, dream activity (REM sleep) and other "automatic" functions like organ function, digestion, hair growth, cellular reproduction and a multitude of other naturally occurring phenomenon are regulated by the subconscious mind.

There is still a great deal about brain/mind function and capability that is not understood. What has been known for sometime, though, is that we possess the ability to affect — even program — impressions or thoughts into our subconscious minds. In doing this, we engage the power of our mind more fully to function on a higher level than the conscious plane. It pushes mind activity into the realm of the involuntary or automatic.

Our intellect operates in the conscious realm, so our "normal" thinking is associated here. When mind function is pushed into the subconscious, it associates outside of intellect and other "normal" functions. Subconscious mind connects with Infinite Mind, Infinite Intelligence and the All Power. The power of the infinite is then engaged.

Jesus said, *"With man this is impossible, but not with God; all things are possible with God."*[57] Inherently we believe this, but we just can't rationalize it in our conscious mind. It goes beyond what we can conceive or imagine. So we limit our belief system, even considering God, because we just can't imagine the full extent of what's possible. It's at this point that our faith, belief and minds fail us — we hit the brick wall of our limited thinking.

When You Believe

We can break these bonds of limitation if we can *conceive and believe* that a certain thing is possible. When we are able to do this, then we can *achieve* what we previously thought was impossible. As we experience victories, our faith, confidence and belief in what's possible all grow. As new truths and realities are manifested in our lives, we know that the power of the Infinite is at work in our lives. Thus the saying, *"whatever the mind can conceive and believe it can achieve."* It is the connection with the All Power — the Universal Mind — that makes this true.

Believe that you have received it...

Jesus said it even better: *"I tell you the truth, if anyone... does not doubt in his heart but believes that what he says will happen, it will be done for him. Therefore I tell you, whatever you ask for in prayer,* **believe that you have received it**, *and it will be yours."*[58]

When we imagine and *believe that we have received it* and pass that conviction to our subconscious mind — in that moment our dream becomes reality. It may be awhile before we realize it, but the essential part — the *most* important part — is done. *How* it gets done can be left to the subconscious and Universal Mind.

When Jesus taught this principle to his disciples, not only was he sharing this with them as a Great Truth, he was coaching their thinking and training their minds. Scientifically, you might describe it this way: "belief" acts upon the subconscious mind; through belief, formless energy takes material form. In this way, your belief is realized or actualized.

You must *BELIEVE!* With belief, miracles happen. Without belief, nothing happens. A famous quote, normally attributed to Henry Ford, but also to Confucius, the ancient Chinese sage, states it bluntly:

"If you think you can, or think you can't — you are right!"

The hit song recorded by Whitney Houston in the 1990's states, *"There will be miracles, when you believe..."* This must be considered one of the most inspiring songs in the modern music era. When we hear those words, we inherently believe them. It makes a deep soul connection that resonates within us. We see and hear similar messages are all around us in music, poetry, movies, etc. Like I said in the Introduction, we hear the words "anything is possible" often. We may even believe it's true. But are we *acting on it* to make it true in our lives? Most of us are not.

Infinite Intelligence gave you the gift of a phenomenal mind with incredible power. We are certainly capable of achieving our hopes and visions (dreams) if we will simply put our *minds* to it. Now, let's get practical and talk about how.

First Step — Visualize

The first and very important step once your desire or dream has been conceived is to create a picture of it in your mind — to **visualize it**. To visualize is a powerful exercise where you begin to imagine yourself actually realizing your dream or vision. Taking this mental action means you are choosing to believe with all your heart and mind that you can attain it.

You must *see yourself* experiencing what you have conceived. Not only do you want to see yourself achieving your dream, you want to *feel it* happening as well. When your visions are emotionalized through your mental pictures, not only do you imagine the experience being manifested, you experience the feelings associated with your objective. In this way you sow the seeds of realizing your dream in your subconscious mind, which then begin to germinate and grow (manifest). This is a powerful process that can be learned and mastered.

> *"Thoughts which are emotionalized are dramatized into experience by the subconscious mind. Your subconscious mind will take your greatest desires or greatest fears as a request and manifest them on the screen of space. What we sow, we shall surely reap."*[59] — *Dr. Joseph Murphy*

Dr. Murphy published a number of landmark books on the workings of the subconscious mind and was a thought leader who taught on the subject around the world for five decades. In case after case, he proved that we could synchronize our conscious and subconscious minds to manifest health, love, wealth, peace or other desires into our lives. He married science with spirituality in his lectures and books through practical application.

The process of *visualizing* **your dream (focused desire) manifests the *materialization* of it**. Here are several practical ways to implement this mental process:

1. **Concentrated Visualization** — In a quiet, relaxed or meditative state, close your eyes and picture a vision of your dream in your mind. See yourself in your ideal place; imagine yourself acting in the capacity of your dream. Feel the emotions, thrills or exhilaration of your experience in your dream vision. See yourself achieving your ideal objective. Make a regular practice of this exercise.

2. **Memory Trigger Visualization** — Use a memory trigger (such as your Dream Necklace) as a reminder to visualize your dream. Each time you see or feel your memory trigger, you are reminded to picture your dream, focus on it and feel yourself experiencing and achieving it.

3. **Picture It** — Draw a picture of your dream. I call these "Dream Scenes." Your picture can be grand and complex or nothing

more than simple stick figures — you do *not* have to be a skilled artist to do this. (I'm still drawing stick figures, but It works for me!) The point is that you're drawing a material representation of you achieving or experiencing your dream. The fact that you're doing this with your own hand drives it deep into your subconscious mind. Whatever is manifested in your subconscious mind can be manifested in your life. When finished, place it in a prominent place where you will see it several times a day and be reminded to visualize and focus on your dream.

4. **Dream/Vision Board** — Using magazines, photos, catalogs or other available images, cut out pictures of things associated or connected with your dream. I suggest starting with a large piece of poster board so you have room to create the vision you want. Again, it can be as simple or complex as you like. Mark on it, add handwritten messages, reminders or labels if you want; enhance by adding your own hand-drawn pictures, or modify the ones you pick. It's *your vision* — make it whatever *you* like! When finished, place it in a prominent place where you'll see it every day (the more often the better), and focus on the dream you envision.

When you create a positive vision of what you want in your conscious imagination and transfer it to your subconscious mind, you begin to manifest its reality. Your subconscious mind connects to the Universal Mind to bring your dreams and visions into reality. The good news is that you have the absolute ability to choose your thoughts, visions and desires — your *Dreams!*

Second Step — Make a Choice

Positive thought generates positive attitudes, life behaviors and outcomes. Habitually negative or fearful thoughts generate destructive and negative emotions and life outcomes. Few of us realize the incredible power we possess in our mind. It is our greatest power and our greatest resource. Through the mind we have access to Infinite Intelligence. Plus, we have the incredible privilege of choice! We have a choice in how we think or respond to any and every situation. We can choose the very course of our lives. What freedom! What power! What authority! Hallelujah!

> *They marveled and glorified God, who had given such power to men.*[60]

What will we do with this incredible freedom? What will we make of it? Make the *most* of it! Make it count! Make it great! For, what goes on in our mind determines who we are and who we shall become. *For as a person thinks in their heart, so they become.*

The Author of Life tells us to think positive thoughts because he knows how powerful our thoughts really are. Because how we think is how we become, we are coached to take captive our thoughts and make them obedient to what is right. He literally tells us to think about what is true, what is right, what is noble, what is pure, what is lovely, what is excellent and worthy of praise —to think about such things.[61] When we do as The Highest Power instructs (the true definition of spirituality), we experience peace, joy and success on a level not equaled elsewhere.

Today most people choose either science or spirituality. Instead, we should combine the two. If you want to bring your dreams into reality, combine the scientific power of the mind with the spiritual power of the Almighty. If you treat one as exclusive of the other, *do not* expect fast results. Infinite Intelligence made the human mind a magnificently powerful control center. Use the gift of your mind to reach your full potential. If you refuse to use what you've been given, you'll lose what you've been given. Jesus illustrated this principle in the Parable of The Talents:

> *"Take the talent from him and give it to the one who has the ten talents. For everyone who has will be given more and he will have abundance. Whoever does not have, even what he has will be taken from him."[62]*

Keep the context in mind here. The one who the talent (a unit of money[63]) was taken from, was lazy and squandered his opportunity to invest or put it to work; whereas the one who had "ten talents" had started with five and gained five more by utilizing and investing what he had been given. In the same way, if we don't use what we're given (our gifts and "talents" — the double meaning being pertinent here), at a minimum we are limiting ourselves. Worse, we may be irresponsible, wasteful or downright lazy. If this is true, we may lose them altogether if we're not stripped of them first.

> *If you refuse to use what you've been given, you'll lose what you've been given.*

So it is with the power of the mind. When we exercise our mental capacities, we strengthen and sharpen our minds. Just like exercising a muscle, greater use creates greater strength. Lack of it dulls your mind. Excessive television watching, for example, dulls our minds. Mental laziness leads to mental weakness. All mind input produces effect. Music, for example, has effect. If we listen to harsh, hard or violent music, it will affect our outlook, attitude and behavior.

Violent movies, video games or other images also affect us. Like food affects our bodies, so the images we feed our minds affect our thoughts, attitudes and behaviors.

We can also positively affect our mental state. Complex classical music, such as Mozart, has been proven to build brain synapse connections. Certain games and puzzle-solving exercises act as mind exercise, sharpening mental acuity. New research claims that certain video games help develop multi-tasking abilities in the brain. Cognitive development exercises with infants and young children aid in building brain function, recognition, comprehension and attention span. Reading is one of the most beneficial forms of mental exercise. Avid readers have higher IQ levels, better vocabularies, increased concentration abilities and comprehension levels. Physical activity such as play and exercise, and a beneficial diet have also proven to benefit our mental condition.

We become the product of what we regularly feed ourselves. Whatever we consistently feed our minds will be faithfully reproduced. So we must choose carefully the "diet" we feed our minds.

Brain Works

Let's look at some aspects of how the brain works:

BRAINWAVE FACTS

Electroencephalography (EEG) is a study of changing electrical potential of the brain. The apparatus used to measure this electric potential of the brain is called electroencephalograph. The tracing or the printout of the measured brainwave forms is electroencephalogram.

Frequency is the number of complete repetitive waves that occur in a given unit of time. Frequency is measured in Hertz (Hz) or cycles per second (cps). According to their frequency brainwaves are divided into four main groups, referred to as "brain states":

EEG Brainwave Sample	Brainwave Frequency	State of Consciousness
	Beta 14 - 40 cps	Fully Awake and Alert. Generally associated with left-brain thinking activity - conscious mind
	Alpha 8 - 13 cps	Relaxed, Daydreaming. Generally associated with right-brain thinking activity - subconscious mind - a key state for "relaxation."
	Theta 4 - 7 cps	Deeply Relaxed, Dreaming. Generally associated with right-brain thinking activity - deeper subconscious to super-conscious. Access to insights, bursts of creativity - a key state for "reality creation" through vivid imagery.
	Delta 0.5 - 3.5 cps	Dreamless. Generally associated with no thinking - unconscious / super-conscious. Access to non-physical states of existence - a key state for healing, "regeneration" and "rejuvenation."

Additional research has been done associated with the activities and benefits of other brainwave frequencies, such as Super Beta, Gamma, etc.

The lower your brainwave cps, the more your awareness is turned toward your subjective experience (subconscious mind), toward your inner world and the more effectively you are able to use the power of your mind to create changes in your body. With each lower state you become more fully aligned with the source of power within you and with Infinite Intelligence, through your subconscious mind.

When you watch television your brain goes into the Alpha state, then into Theta, and possibly into the Delta state. TV advertisers pay over 70 billion dollars per year to take advantage of these deeper hypnotic brain states to plant their product images into your deeper mind. They invest in the hope that when your brain is later in the active Beta (conscious) state, your subconscious mind recalls the advertised product(s) and directs your conscious mind to purchase them. This is especially effective with children, teenagers and young adults who are unaware of this phenomenon.

Generally in the Beta State, your attention is focused outward. In the Alpha state your attention begins to turn inward. In Theta and Delta your attention goes further and further inward to your deeper mind, the subconscious mind.

At the borderline between Beta and Alpha States is a doorway to your subconscious mind. This doorway consists of what hypnosis refers to as your "critical faculty."

At the borderline between Alpha and Theta states is a doorway to your super-conscious mind, where you begin to gain access to "supernatural abilities." This is the state that your brain goes into when you are in deep meditation. The more time you spend in this state, the more these "abilities" become a part of you. Bursts of insight and connection with the Higher Power are experienced by most while in this meditative state.

At the borderline between Theta and Delta, you begin to experience non-physical consciousness. Manifesting changes in your outer world is powerful in this state, because you transcend physical consciousness and make a deep connection with the subconscious mind. This state is also where you enter the dream state and where REM (rapid eye movement) sleep occurs. Dreams are physically active, vivid and quite real in this state.

The Delta state is a deep, dreamless state where your mind is fully resting. Your body has the best opportunity to regenerate in this state. Those practiced in meditation can develop the ability to remain conscious while getting progressively into deeper and deeper states. A person without any mind training will tend to fall asleep when getting into theta state, while a person who has undergone some form of meditative mind-training will be able to be very deeply relaxed, yet conscious. The more you are able to remain conscious while in deeper states of mind, the less sleep you will require, because both your mind and body are able to reach deep restful states.[64]

I make a practice of utilizing these super-conscious brain states as I'm falling asleep at night, waking up in the morning and having my meditation times each day. It is during these times that I'm focused on manifesting my dreams and visions. As I've mentioned, this has worked very successfully for me over the last 24 years and for my clients as well.

Albert Einstein was well known for utilizing the brain state that bordered the Alpha and Theta states. He rested regularly with afternoon naps or periods of quiet meditation. This is what some researchers refer to as the "genius state" — where flashes of inspiration, ideas and insights occur. Could it be that periods of prayer or meditation can induce the "genius" in us? We believe that to be true. This is where our subconscious mind connects with the Universal Mind — the Mind of God. He can give us ideas and flashes of genius too, because there is an Einstein in each of us. Just as Albert Einstein exercised this practice and became better at it over the years, so can you.

Step Three — Directed Thought Energy

When we learn to harness our thought energy and focus its direction, we learn to proactively use the power of our mind capacity. It has been scientifically proven that we actually project energy with our thoughts.[65] We become what we think about. Our lives are a manifestation of our thoughts. Our thoughts definitely have this kind of power whether you accept this fact or not. Thoughts absolutely become things. This is the **Power of the Mind**.

> *"Scientists are just beginning to accept the truth about thought energy, and have begun to study what many have known for centuries. In fact some of today's leading scientists in areas of physics, biology, psychology and many other fields are starting to recognize the importance of thought energy." — Dr. Jeffry Palmer, PhD*

I was fascinated to find that a new game had been created recently by Hammacher Schlemmer, which actually captures, focuses and directs the energy of thought. The game is called "Mind Flex" and the player wears a headpiece that captures theta brain waves and directs their energy to a receiver.[66] The object of the game is to use concentrated thought energy to direct a ball through a "telekinetic obstacle course" with your mind! Amazing!

Hammacher Schlemmer's Telekinetic Obstacle Course Game called "Mind Flex"

In navigating the obstacle course of life, thought energy works in both directions — positive or negative. If you are full of gratitude, encouragement and optimism, things will positively and joyfully manifest for you. If your mind is pre-occupied with fear and failure, you will manifest what you fear and experience failure.

"Few understand or appreciate the vast storehouse of knowledge and power of the subconscious mind, and that it can be drawn upon at will. Through intense concentration or active desire we penetrate to the realm of the subconscious and register our thought upon it. Such thoughts are invariably realized. The trouble is that it is often our negative thoughts — our fears — that penetrate. And these are realized just as surely as the positive thoughts."[67] — Robert Collier

Again this demonstrates the principle that *as we think, so we become.* This is a function of the subconscious mind. We must realize that we possess incredible personal power, which has been given to us from On High. We must accept responsibility for this power, learn to harness it and direct it positively and productively.

I'm sure you know someone who is hopelessly negative. They're always down. Hardship and trouble seem to follow them around. It could be illness, car trouble or they just lost their wallet. They're always sick, always broke — on and on it goes. It's stifling and upsetting to even be *around* a person like this because it's like a contagious disease! You can easily be pulled into their negative cycle.

On the other hand, we probably know people that everything seems to go great for. Great new job, promotion, came into a great business deal, etc. There is always something positive or exciting going on in their lives, they're always winning and things just seem to go well for them all the time.

What's the difference? I believe it's their thinking. One is focused on negative thinking, the other on positive. One draws negative events and actions into their life, the other positive.

"What you think about expands." — Dr. Wayne Dyer

Positive Replacement

Negative thinking is a chain that can be broken, but you must deliberately train your mind to the positive. You must learn to take captive negative thoughts and turn them into positive, healthy thoughts. I call this "**Positive Replacement**." This is how you begin to break the chain and it is a discipline that can be learned. Most of us need to be trained in it, however.

Eliminate negatives in thought and action, actively replacing them with working positives — this is Positive Replacement.

It is not effective just to focus on *eliminating negatives* in your life. We need to actively *replace* them with working positives if we want changes to be successful and permanent. This could mean thought patterns, lifestyle habits or other life conditions. You must not only stop doing what is negative or destructive, you must start doing what is positive and constructive. An alcoholic, for example, needs not only to stop drinking, they must also replace that behavior with healthy habits and activities. The void must be filled with something else that is good and right. Let me give you some examples:

- You want to **quit smoking**. First, you must address your thought. You don't say "I will quit smoking, I will quit smoking, I will quit smoking!" By doing this, you are drilling "smoking" into your mind all the more. Instead, create a positive replacement by saying something like "My lungs are healthy and clear." You don't even want to say "I am smoke free." Why? Because you're still focused on "smoke." Replace all negative thoughts with positive equivalents. Then put action behind these thoughts.

- You want to **lose weight**. In the same way, you don't say "I want to lose weight." If you do, you'll stay focused on "weight." Instead, you say "I am lean and fit" or "I eat only fresh and healthy foods" or "I love to exercise 5-6 times a week" or maybe all of the above. Focus on the positive. Visualize the result you want. Eliminate the negative from both your thought patterns and your daily actions. Then begin to do the things that will accomplish the change you seek.

- You want a **new job**. Perhaps you've been unemployed or underemployed for a length of time. First, you must stop thinking "*unemployed.*" Erase that word from your vocabulary and therefore your subconscious mind. Don't tell yourself "times are tough" or "there are no jobs" or "this is a bad economy" and all things like it. Manage your self-talk, because if you tell yourself or others those things, they will be true for you. Begin telling yourself "I have a great new job in _____" (work type/area of choice) or "I love my new _____ job!" Visualize the results you want. Follow these positive thoughts up with the actions that accompany them and it will manifest in your life.

Create positive statements for what you desire. Then *act* on these statements. This is where most people fall short — they don't act! What you desire will not fall from the sky. You must actively *seek it!* Seek and you will find it; knock and the door will be opened to you; ask and you will receive it.[68]

Ask for it. Go get it! Act as if you already have it. Visualize it. Build it into your life. Put actions behind your thoughts and *it will manifest*.

Everyone who asks receives; those who seek find; those who knock, the door will be opened to them — this is a promise of God!

The concept of Positive Replacement is demonstrated well by Emmet Fox in his book, The Mental Equivalent.

> "To change your thought and keep it changed is to build a new mental equivalent; it is the secret to accomplishment. You already have a mental equivalent for everything in your life today; you must destroy the patterns of the things you do not want and they will disappear. You must build a new pattern or mental equivalent for the things you want, then they will come into your life." — Emmet Fox

Napoleon Hill taught a method he referred to as "conscious auto-suggestion,"[69] which means to consciously suggest the desired outcome or result to your subconscious mind. Based on Mr. Hill's extensive life work, he advised that you should affirm it repeatedly twice daily.[70] In this way faith is put to work with action and the expectation of it becoming reality. This method works incredibly well. When such methods are mastered and you learn to direct your thought energy, the desired results you seek will inevitably manifest.

When Jesus taught us to *believe that we have received it*, he was teaching us to understand and master the *most essential* element of our mental capacity — we can manifest new realities with faithful expectancy. It is not wrong to use it. We are the ones who suffer (and those dependent on us) if we do not. I believe this is primarily how we *will do even greater things*.[71] As he taught his disciples then, so he is teaching us today how to use the power of our minds. Those everywhere who love and believe in God, especially Christians, should embrace these important truths. They only hurt and limit themselves if they do not.

Your mind has incredible power. Simply put, the subconscious mind is the most powerful life force you possess. Thought energy is one of the only elements that you have direct control over. When you learn to properly direct your thoughts, it enables you to harness the power of your mind. If practiced regularly, you can master these methods and put them to work for you in meaningful ways.

It only takes 21 days to form a new habit. Commit to train your mind and your thinking, cancelling negative thoughts and actively substituting them with Positive Replacement. Do this for 21 consecutive days and you'll be amazed at the results you experience.

As you learn to master and direct your thoughts, you will positively influence all areas of your life. To do so, you must first acknowledge, embrace and learn to use the Power of the Mind that God gave you. It is your most important asset and what sets you apart in all known creation. It enables you to connect to the Universal Mind and Infinite Intelligence. With your mind properly trained, you can positively and proactively direct the outcomes of your life, and ultimately direct your destiny.

Practical: Practice Positive Replacement. Identify one to three negative behaviors in your life that continue to challenge you or cause you problems. Choose to replace the negative thought patterns with working positives for 21 consecutive days. This could involve thoughts, words (how you speak about yourself of circumstances) or things that you do (behaviors).

Support this practice with written affirmations, which you will speak out loud morning and evening, when you rise and before sleep. Capture negative thoughts, if they occur, and replace them with a suitable positive.

Reality TV Bite: When we filmed the show, there was a small production crew at each location. In each case, the members of the crew were fascinated with the concept of manifesting. Separate from the show content, they asked about it off camera frequently. What was interesting is that over the two-week duration of filming the show, we started to see examples of certain things manifesting among the crew. We would talk about something, they'd think about it, and a day or two later it just seemed to happen. My husband and I would then point it out and they'd be amazed. Eventually, several of the crewmembers shared personal examples of things that had manifested in their lives. It was fun to see, discuss and experience. We hope each of them has taken a little piece of that with them, or will perhaps become Dream Program clients in the future.

Remember: If you feel you need personal mentoring, coaching and guidance through these or any exercises that are part of the Dream Program visit www.DreamProgram.com/store.

Chapter 7

The Power of Passion

Passion: 1. a powerful or compelling emotion or feeling 2. a strong or extravagant fondness, enthusiasm, or desire for anything 3. the object of such a fondness or desire

We each possess the incredible Power of Passion. It is a *burning desire* within us powered by the Human Spirit. Passion is the spark that ignites the fire within our hearts. When we are *passionate* about something, there is an extra energy that drives us — a supernatural energy. Passion is the fuel for our engine. It is the adrenaline that propels us long after others have quit or failed. Passion is driven by love, for what we truly love we are very passionate about.

"No power within man is as great as that of passion... a burning desire!" — Napoleon Hill

In each of our hearts, passion fans the flames of our dreams. They are different for each of us. God placed them there. Not only did he place them there, he planted them in us with the intention that they should be nurtured to grow and ultimately be realized. In Napoleon Hill's landmark work, *Think & Grow Rich*, he states:

"You would not have your desires and passions if you were not capable of their achievement."

This statement was so important that Mr. Hill described it as the summation of all he had learned in a lifetime devoted to research and study of phenomenally successful people, many of whom made history with their achievements. It is incredibly important to grasp this concept. If we do not understand this, we are likely to wander in the mediocrity of an unfulfilling existence, or empty, pointless work.

Sadly, far too many of us are not passionate about what we do at all. We've been conditioned to think certain ways about what we should do when we grow up — either by culture, society, parents or schooling. Have you ever known someone who was miserable doing what they did — even if they were successful — but they kept doing it because it was all they knew? Or perhaps you've known someone afraid to leave a "secure" job in order to break away to do what they desire in their heart instead?

My dad was a perfect example. His name was **Farid Fuleihan**. He immigrated here as a young man from Jordan to pursue a medical career, and eventually became a very prominent and successful surgeon. The problem was, even though he was successful, he didn't like it. He made lots of money, had a beautiful home in an affluent suburb, had a lake house and all the trappings of success. But he wasn't happy. Dad loved to cook and he was fabulous at it! He loved being in the kitchen and he'd always talk about opening his own restaurant. He might have been an incredible chef and even more importantly — he may have been extremely happy doing this. But he never did it. He was afraid to leave his successful career as a surgeon — and who could blame him? If he had, everyone would've told him he was crazy! That's the way our society has conditioned us to think. "A surgeon becomes a chef? Is he nuts?!"

Unfortunately, Dad never acted on his dream. He died suddenly and tragically of a massive heart attack while visiting my older brother several years ago. He was only 60 years old. Ironically, it happened in a restaurant. His dream died with him. He was "successful" but he wasn't happy. His success actually trapped him. I believe the stress of his "success" and the pressure to maintain it may have actually killed him.

What if he had left medicine and made the jump to the restaurant business? He surely would've taken a pay cut. What if he made less than half or even one-third of what he had been making before? "Disaster" you say? But what if he was *happy* doing it? What if he *loved* going to work every day and couldn't wait to get there? Maybe he would've been "successful" in a different way, or maybe he would've struggled. How do you define success? If he was fulfilled and living with passion that would matter for something, wouldn't it?

Our culture places far too much emphasis on money. We worship it. It is a "god" to many of us. This is modern day idolatry. It's not a statue, but it is an object of worship. If we love money, we'll never have enough of it.[72] If we pursue it, we may get it, but only at great cost. Deep down we know these things, but we are easily blinded to them. Make no mistake about it, the forces of evil know these truths as well and use them very effectively to make us fall. So we must disarm the evil one by aligning ourselves and our ambitions with God and his perfect Word.

We must be true to ourselves and pursue our passions. Our healthy desires and passions have been planted in our hearts for a reason. They are there by design. The Infinite One wants you to act on them in your life but he doesn't stop there. He wants to give you the desires of your heart. He has incredible plans for your life. He wants to bless you and wants you to prosper. He wants you to have even more than you ask for or imagine.[73] This is part of the "all" that he has promised you.

If we do what we're passionate about, the money will come! Passion rules, passion persuades, passion sells... passion is *POWERFUL!* Unite your passions with your business pursuits and you will be successful. Consider the inspiring story of Edward Beauvais, my father-in-law.

Edward "Ed" Beauvais grew up in a Southern Colorado steel-mill town where the whistle blew every morning at 6 a.m. for the morning shift change. The steelworkers were mostly Slovinians, Italians and Irish Catholics who migrated to this blue-collar town after World War I. His father was an accountant at the mill and worked there most of his life.

A gifted athlete, Ed went to college on a football scholarship when most in his hometown went to work at the mill. Homesick and missing Mary Ellen, the high school sweetheart he would later marry, he transferred back to Regis College in Denver in during his second year. Regis had dropped football, so Ed switched to baseball instead.

He married Mary Ellen before his senior year, and worked at a CPA firm while finishing an accounting degree. After graduation they returned to their hometown and Ed took a job at the mill in the accounting department. When a college buddy later contacted him about a finance job with small Denver-based Frontier Airlines, he faced a difficult choice. He was excited about the airline job opportunity, but his family, everyone at the mill and in his hometown thought he was crazy to leave a "good job" to work in the fledgling airline industry. After careful thought, Ed decided to step out of his hometown comfort zone and take the airline job in nearby Denver.

This magnified a few years later when he learned that Las Vegas based Bonanza Airlines was looking for someone in his field. It was the early 1960's and Las Vegas was a dusty little desert gambling town, plus the airline industry was considered unproven and unstable. Now Ed was considering a move far from home. Against family advice he accepted the new job and moved his young family to Nevada.

At Bonanza, Ed moved from accounting into planning and development, setting company growth strategy. He excelled in this role and moved to larger companies and higher-ranking positions. He was an Assistant VP at San Francisco-based AirWest when Howard Hughes made a hostile bid and bought the company. Hughes' management team wanted Ed to stay on, but he left to start his own consulting firm, which he ran successfully through the

1970's. Many of his former "bosses" went to work for him at the consulting firm.

When the airline industry was deregulated in 1978, Ed saw great opportunity in the western U.S. Sunbelt. He anticipated the growth of Phoenix, Arizona and began planning a new airline headquartered there. In 1980 he began work on **America West Airlines**, building his business plan, management team and obtaining seed capital. Ed was confident and optimistic in spite of the skeptics. Nothing deterred him. He was so passionate in communicating his vision that he gained wide support from influential leaders. After a successful 22 million dollar IPO, he launched the company in 1983.

With the help of his employees, Ed built **America West** into a **1.3 billion dollar airline** and **created over 15,000 jobs**. Amazing! Today it flies as **USAirways**, having acquired its larger competitor in 2005. Ed also started Western Pacific Airlines and Mountain Air Express, which he has since sold his interests in.

Imagine if he stayed in his hometown, with his "stable" and "secure" job at the steel mill. Thank God he didn't because he changed so many lives by pursuing his vision with courage and undying optimism. What looked 'solid as steel' back then has been very unstable for more than 40 years. Instead he had the courage to challenge conventional norms and step out of the comfort zone his friends and family advised him to stay in. He certainly contributed to the common good by using his natural resources — his gifts, talents and passions.

It will *always* take courage to pursue your dreams. Many times those closest to you will *not* be supportive. They may even be critical, skeptical and doubtful, trying to convince you to do what's "sensible," "safe" or "secure." When your ideas are in their infancy, choose the people you share them with very carefully. That is when your ideas are most vulnerable, and you must protect them from criticism and attack. Often the members of our own families are the biggest "dream killers." Ed's story is an inspiring example of what can be achieved when you don't listen to the naysayers and decide to go after your dreams with passion.

Reality TV Bite: When my husband and I were first being interviewed on camera by the Reality TV television show producer for the initial two days, he asked me, "You must be willing to be a martyr to be on this show. Are you?" I thought to myself, what am I so passionate about that I'm willing to die for? My answer was "Dream to Destiny." It is how I live and who I am. If people don't like it, too bad — it's their loss. Our passion for The Dream Program is the main reason we were chosen to do the show. If you are truly passionate about something, you won't be concerned with what others think.

Love is the Key!

What do you absolutely *LOVE?* I mean you love, love, love it! Love is the key. The things you love hold the key to your heart and mind. Whatever they are, the things you love, the things you're *passionate* about, *those* things show you the way you should go. Whatever "it" is, you should center your professional life around it — your career, your pursuits, your expertise and your business. You are obsessed with it anyway. Why not make it generate income for you? In this way, your hobby can become your profession.

If you're not sure what the "it" is for you, here are some clues:

- You lose all track of time when doing it
- You'd do it for free, just because you love doing it
- You feel a supreme sense of satisfaction when you do it well
- You are compelled, maybe even obsessed with getting better at it
- You love showing others how to do it or telling them about it
- You could do it all night, denying yourself sleep or other necessities
- You wake up thinking about it or have dreams about it

There may be other measures, but these are a few. If three or more of these are true about a healthy thing or pursuit in your life, it's a strong indication of your passion for it.

When you do what you love, you will love getting up
every day to do it!

When you make your passion your profession, you can become the best in the world at it. This does not mean the best in the *entire* world. It means the best in *your* world. Each of us can be the best in the world at something. The "world" can be measured as a neighborhood, a town, a state, a region, the country, etc. You get the idea.

Do you want to be "good" at something, or do you want to be "great" at it? If we love something, we will love learning about it, we'll be fascinated by it and always find it interesting. When we're passionate about something, others can tell because we are engaging and compelling when talking about it. Passion paints word pictures, passion persuades and passion sells. Passion is the KEY to greatness! People LOVE working with those who are passionate about what they do. They are drawn by it like a magnet. It's impossible to compete against Passion or Love.

Your "Niche"

If you want to be great at what you do, discover your passions and gifts (your "Loves") and excel in them. Plan your life around them. The diagram below of The 3 Circles™ is a helpful guide to finding your greatness. The first circle represents your **Gifts and Talents**, the second your **Dreams and Passions,** and the third is **Economic Opportunities**.

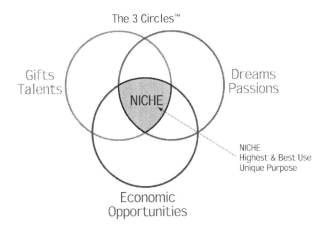

This is a very helpful exercise you'll want to spend some time on. Review your findings from the DTQ. Use the "Gift List" if it will be helpful for you. Make an exhaustive list of your Gifts and Talents. Then make a detailed list of your Dreams and Passions. Take your time and make sure to be thorough. Finally, brainstorm Economic Opportunities. There are *always* opportunities, no matter where you are or what the local conditions are. It's a good idea to get outside input in the form of a "Mastermind Group" for this.[74] (Make sure you choose positive-minded people for your brainstorming or mastermind group.)

As you complete this exercise, work toward the middle — the "Shield." The area where The 3 Circles intersect is your **"Niche."** This center shield area identifies your area niche, or your area of "highest and best use." This is a vitally important area for each of us, because it identifies your unique purpose. This is who you are *designed* to be.

What is this telling you? Again, it may be helpful to get some outside input (Dream Program coaching is available for you as well[75]) Stay focused and disciplined to stay within The 3 Circles. Say "NO" to opportunities that come up that are not within your niche and you will always be functioning at your highest and best use. Once you identify your niche — your unique purpose — make plans to pursue it. Your highest and best use is your unique purpose. When you function in this zone, you will excel into your greatness and benefit the common good. I am totally convinced that if you work within this space, it will be your "Recession Proof Shield."

*If you work within your **niche**, it will be your*
***recession proof shield**.*

Genuine passion cannot be manufactured. It's either real or it's not. If it's not real you'll just be going through the motions. When you do what you're passionate about, with the gifts that God gave you, ***the money will come!*** You must believe this and not doubt. You may not get rich, you may not live on a mountain top, but you will be fulfilled and happy. You'll love what you do and love your life. Money can't buy these things. This is what success is made of. Ideas are the seeds of greatness when they're powered by passion. Allow yourself to imagine what is needed and passionately create it utilizing your gifts. Your passions, coupled with your gifts, dreams and desires will lead you to true success.

My professional background is in corporate technology sales. Right now, there are opportunities for me to work in that field earning five figures per month. This is something I could do. I'm skilled at it and I know I could be successful in it. But I must be true to myself. It is not my passion. The money is not important enough to me to suggest that I should do something that forces me to sacrifice time with my husband and children for a career I'm not passionate about. I will not do it. Instead, I feel compelled to bring this message of hope and encouragement to you. This is my unique purpose in life for now. I've learned to say "No" to opportunities that are not within my niche so that I can function in my highest and best use.

From Good to Great

The Key to Greatness is to stay focused on your niche, whether personal or professional. In his excellent book *Good to Great*, Stanford professor Tim Collins explains in detail what makes certain companies GREAT. He studied many companies to find out what made them so successful compared to others which had just average performance. What he found was that the great ones stayed focused on what they were best at, what they could be

"World Class" at, and what they could do uniquely better than their competition. He called this their "Hedge Hog Concept" (which is the intersection of The 3 circles in Figure A above). For these companies it was a decision of strategy and focus.

When we as individuals focus on our passions and gifts, we are making the same decisions great companies make. In this way, we're identifying what we can be "World Class" at (remember, in "our world"). Just as a great or highly successful company can excel in their niche, so can we. This becomes our "Hedgehog Concept."

Notice in Figure B below, that the intersection of The 3 circles forms the shape of a shield. There will always be demand for those who are excellent at what they do and stand out from the rest. When you are working in the area of your passions and gifts, you are in your "shield" of excellence, your highest and best use, or what you're best in the world at. This is your *recession proof shield*.

"Shield"

NICHE
Highest & Best Use
Unique
Purpose

Recession-Proof
Shield

Convergence of Opportunity
and Natural Resources

This is our *Niche*. Our niche is our **highest and best use**, where we are most effective and productive. When we learn to identify the characteristics of our niche, we gain the Key to unlock the door of our **unique purpose** in life. We can then step into our **divine destiny**. If we build our life in this space, we will build on a foundation of strength where we can truly be GREAT. We will be doing what we are intended to do — what we are *designed* to do. When we live with passion and purpose we will be happy and fulfilled, living in the area of our gifts, passions and dreams.

Career Choice — Entrepreneur, Professional or Networker

If you have the knack to create your own business, thriving in the area of your passions and gifts, you will be successful. But not everyone is an entrepreneur. For some, their niche is filling a certain role within a company — and this is exactly where they should be. Self-employment is the way to go for others. Licensed professionals such as accountants, contractors, doctors, financial planners, lawyers, mortgage brokers and real estate professionals are some examples.

Many who seek financial independence don't fit neatly into any of these categories, though. For them the opportunities available through network marketing may be their calling.[76] Many fine companies offer an entrepreneurial chance for people to start a business with very little up-front cost, low overhead and virtually unlimited income potential in most cases.

Many a fortune has been made among network marketing professionals. But their fortunes are usually enjoyed quietly, off the radar screen of mainstream media or society. Yet within their company circles, highly successful leaders enjoy the celebrity of a rock star! Most however are humble, modest, down-to-earth and very real people. That's the beauty of it — they are no different from you or me. They just went after something with passion and perseverance and built a successful business for themselves. What is their message to others? YOU can do it too! Talk to any of them, and you will see.

There are many excellent companies and product types to choose from virtually anywhere, around the world. If you're hungry for such an opportunity, you can definitely find one that's right for you. What you should look for is a product you can get behind with passion and utilize your unique gifts. Seek one that is stable and trustworthy with a compensation plan that is unlimited. If you do, then this might be the right entrepreneurial connection for you. With patience, determination and perseverance, you can build a business that creates passive residual income for the rest of your life.

Do Not Settle!

You cannot manufacture passion. You cannot just decide to be passionate about something. It's either there or it isn't. You were designed to live with passion and love what you do. If you compromise this, you may get by or even do well, but you may just be going through the motions of life. DO NOT settle for this type of mediocre existence!

Have the courage to pursue your visions, desires and True Dreams. The passions within your heart and mind are there for a *reason!* They are there with intention and purpose. They are there by design. Trust what God has placed within you, embrace them and become the person you were designed to be! In this way, you will step into your **divine destiny**.

The Power of Passion is the Power of the Human Spirit.

Everything that is good is of God. He wants an intimate two-way relationship with us because we are his precious children. He wants to be closely connected with us. He wants to be ONE with us! His Spirit lives in us and longs to guide us in what is right and best. This is how we are "created in his image" — we are spiritual beings created to be like God in a spiritual sense. The Power of Passion *is* the Power of the Human Spirit. We must not quench the spirit of passion or put its fire out within us. If we let this spirit reign in us, then we will become all we are designed to be.

When you embrace your healthy passions you will function in your niche — your highest and best use. Doors will open for you and opportunities will flow your way. You will shine like a bright star in a dark world. If passion is directing your pursuits, you will excel to your highest level. You will be your Best YOU! When most people are going through the motions, you will be full of Life and Joy. You will achieve your Greatness!

Practical: Complete The 3 Circles diagram exercise. Refer to your DTQ, the Gift List, your journal notes or any other resource that may help you. Complete it initially yourself. Then with the help of a brainstorming partner or mastermind group, get some outside input for further completion. We don't often see ourselves objectively, so we need this help for self-assessment and to brainstorm economic opportunities.

Reality TV Bite: Every scene and situation portrayed on the show, from the arrival to the departure, is a complete surprise. I had no idea where I was even going. I flew from Phoenix to Chicago, connected to an Indiana flight then drove to our final location in Elkhart. Until we pulled into the town, I didn't know where I would end up. From the initial visit to the "swap" family home to our first meeting and throughout the swap, each situation was thrust upon us with little notice or explanation — it all just happened "right now!" The show's sole purpose is to create conflict and spark heated words and emotions. The producers/directors (yes, there are directors) are highly skilled at making these things happen. They aren't really interested in *reality* — their job is to produce interesting television. There were no scripts and no one actually told anyone what to say, but there were plenty of leading questions and remarks off camera that stimulated or provoked the kind of inflammatory comments they wanted and the friction they were looking for. I believe they have a very good idea of what they want before they even begin filming, although each family member involved has no idea what's coming next – from the first day to the very end.

Important: If you feel you need personal mentoring, coaching and guidance through these or any exercises that are part of the Dream Program visit at www.DreamProgram.com/store.

Chapter 8

The Highest Power – The Power of God

The LORD is righteous in all his ways and loving toward all he has made.[77]

By far the greatest power is the Power of God. Nothing transcends the Power of God. Nothing. This may also be the most misunderstood power, at least as far as it pertains to us.

Many of us have an unhealthy or warped view of God. These views may be skewed by harmful religious experiences we've had in our lives, unhealthy or toxic relationships we've had with authority figures — be they parents, relatives, teachers, coaches, clergy or others. Often, people view God in the light of the relationship they have with their earthly father. If that relationship is good and healthy, so is their view of God. If that relationship is unhealthy (which is often the case), their view is embittered or negative.

The factors that can twist our view of God relative to the relationship we have (or had) with our physical fathers may range from absent non-existence to harsh, harmful or downright abusive. If any of these are true we may have to work hard to build a healthy view of our Heavenly Father. We must learn to separate the pain or damage that may have come from our earthly fathers from our relationship with the Almighty Father. God is not like our physical fathers, except perhaps in the best sense.

For I am God, and not man — the Holy One among you.[78]

God is not man. He is not a person exhibiting human tendencies or behaviors — he is holy. He is neither father nor mother, male or female. God is beyond the bounds of our comprehension and perception. He is the omnipotent, omniscient and omnipresent supreme spiritual being. He is the Almighty, Universal, Highest and Infinite Power. He is all-loving, compassionate, gentle, tender, merciful and full of grace. He is patient with us, not wanting anyone to perish but wants everyone to come to a knowledge of the truth and into a relationship with him.[79] We refer to God as "he" because we lack a term in our limited physical language that goes beyond it, so please bear with me as I refer to God as "he" or "him" or "Father" in the male vernacular.

It is essential that we understand that God loves us. I mean he *LOVES* us! More than we know, more than we can even imagine. He is the perfect parent. He wants to bless you. He wants you to be joyful, peaceful and fulfilled. He knows what's best for you. This is beautifully demonstrated in the following scripture:

"For I know the plans I have for you," declares the LORD, "plans to prosper you and not to harm you, plans to give you a hope and a future."[80]

God has great plans for you and your life! Plus, he has the ability to make anything happen — *anything!* He wants you to trust him and ask for his help. He wants you to rely on him and not on inferior things. With The Power of God on your side, *anything is possible!* You need only to ask and believe. God is faithful to his promises and always keeps them. This is a fact on which you can fully rely.

There Will Be Miracles...

If you *do not* believe that miracles can happen for you, then miracles *will not* happen for you. A great example of this is shown when Jesus returns to his hometown of Nazareth after beginning his public ministry. (This account is found in Mark 6:1-6) On the Sabbath he began to teach in the local synagogue. Instead of being filled with faith, all the locals could think about was who he had been:

"Where did this man get these things? What's this wisdom that has been given him... Isn't this the carpenter? Isn't this Mary's son?..." And they took offense at him.

Jesus said to them, "Only in his hometown, among his relatives and in his own house is a prophet without honor." He could not do any miracles there... and he was amazed at their lack of faith.

All they could see was the carpenter who grew up down the street. They refused to believe and even "took offense at him." Often, our own family members are the least supportive or last to believe us. Do not be surprised if this happens in your life, because if it happened to the Lord, it could happen to you. The gospels are full of miracle accounts based on people's faith. Unfortunately for those in Nazareth, their *lack of faith* denied them the miracles that may have been done in their lives.

With man this is impossible, but with God all things are possible.[81]

Nothing is impossible for the Infinite One. Nothing! Jesus said, "If you have faith and do not doubt... If you believe, you will receive whatever you ask for in prayer."[82] I believe that Jesus himself manifested the miracles he performed through a pure, total and absolute faith. It wasn't magical power; it was the Power of God working through his faith. He described it this way: "Rather, it is the Father, living in me, doing his work... at least believe on the evidence of the miracles themselves."[83] He goes on to say, "I tell you the truth, anyone who has faith in me will do what I have been doing. He will do even *greater* things..."[84] (emphasis mine). Consider the weight of this statement — we will do even *greater* things than Jesus himself! How can that be? According to our faith it will be done. When we put our faith and trust in The Highest Power, anything is possible. We can move mountainous problems and challenges in our lives with a tiny seed of faith.[85] We take the first step of faith and the Infinite One does the rest.

There is actually no way of overstating God's Power — the Infinite One is ALL-Powerful![86] Our faith is a factor — a strong factor. When we focus our faith with the Power of our Mind (our thinking and mindset), driven by the Power of our Passions (the Human Spirit) and combine this with the Power of God, this tri-union gives you an unstoppable advantage. Anything is possible. New realities can be created or manifested in your life. Hearts and minds can change. Miracles can happen. Your dreams can become your destiny.

Time for Change

In **June of 1992** I was done with the bar scene along with superficial friends and boyfriends. I had a strong desire for REAL friends that loved me for who I was. I was desperate to break the chains of dysfunction passed down to me through generations — cursing, smoking, drunkenness, immorality and the like. The Mighty One was working in me to will and to act according to his good purpose.[87] He was changing my heart so that my desires were becoming right and healthy. Attentive to his promptings, I took action.

Engaging the power of my subconscious mind, I handwrote a list of the 10 positive affirmations I wanted to manifest. Here's what I handwrote on a note pad: "I am fit for life loving healthy food. Only good words come out of my mouth (no more cursing). I love my sober state of mind. I have unconditionally loving friends. I wait until I get married to have sex. I belong to a church that lives by the Bible and the members are truly loving. I am a successful entrepreneur..." (there were more). Every night sitting in bed before falling asleep I prayed over my list, knowing it would sink deep into my subconscious mind and help bring these desires into my reality. When my alarm went off in the morning I reached over, grabbed this list and prayed over it again. (Without being fully aware of it at the time, I was employing **The 3 Powers™ simultaneously!**)

A short time later, while I was at a doctor's appointment a pretty girl named Caroline invited me to her church. When I went to church with her, I was amazed. This was the answer to my prayers and a manifestation of my dream. Some great women studied the Bible with me over the next few weeks, teaching me the Scriptures and how to apply them to my life. They taught me how to tap into the Power of God. It radically changed my life! I was baptized and knew exactly why I was doing it. My heart, mind and soul have been transformed ever since that Sunday — September 13, 1992. The desire to get drunk, do drugs, smoke cigarettes, curse and be sexually immoral were removed from my mind and heart because of the positive truths now replacing the negative thoughts. (This is a terrific example of "Positive Replacement.") My mind was made new. The good thoughts turned into good desires, which became good habits, which led to good character traits, which have become my destiny. **Every single dream on my list became my reality within three months.** It happened so fast because I simultaneously applied The 3 Powers. My heart, mind and soul were renewed, thanks be to God!

To this day (more than 17 years later) I am eternally grateful to my Heavenly Father who worked in those women's hearts to help me and teach me how to apply his Word to my life. Since then I have lived a fulfilled, prosperous and successful life. We live in a world of overflowing abundance. God created it that way for us. If you persistently go after your desires in connection with the Infinite One, you will receive them. It comes down to your faith and action. As it clearly states in the book of James, "I will show you my faith by what I do" and "faith without deeds is useless."[88] You must take action if your dreams are to come true.

This is not a prosperity gospel. I went after what I wanted (mentally, passionately and spiritually) and got it. Physical efforts are of some value, but I believe spiritual efforts are actually more "efficient." (When you employ The 3 Powers simultaneously, your dreams manifest.) God *wants* to bless us with the desires of our hearts. If you have a burning desire to be financially free, you've been given that desire for a reason. Financial freedom is one of my desires because I want to be there for my children when they come home from school. The way I look at it is that I have one chance to raise my children and to give them a happy childhood. No matter what, I will be here for my kids and my husband because I'm deeply passionate about them. I will be my very best for them by utilizing my gifts, talents and passions to create a full-time income working around our family schedule. God has blessed this desire.

Reality TV Bite: My husband and I went through many extensive interviews, background checks, blood tests and psychological tests (including our children) over several months to get the spot on "Wife

Swap." Because we had The 3 Powers working for us, God opened all the doors and we flew through them with ease. We asked him for the opportunity with complete faith, took action and he delivered. We then relied on him every step of the way during the two weeks of filming. Now we are relying on him along with the other two Powers (Mind and Passion) to help us after the show premieres and plays in syndication for the next three to four years on "Lifetime" and other networks. We are literally walking in faith and trust.

Heart Change

We must guard our hearts from desires and dreams that are materialistic or selfish in nature. The Infinite One has placed healthy desires on our hearts for a reason, to fulfill his dream, purpose and destiny for our lives. However, he gives us choices. We are ultimately the ones who decide the direction and destiny of our lives based on what we choose. If we chase unhealthy pursuits we may get what we want, but we'll reap the consequences that accompany them. If we stay connected in communication with God though, things will change. Our desires will change. New opportunities will appear before us. Doors will open for us. God will change our hearts. What we want will change. We will change. God will not *make* us do anything, but he will guide us in these ways to what is right and best for us. This is the Power of God working in us. It is up to us to follow the path and walk through the doors he opens.

The key is to do some deep soul searching with the help of our DTQ so that you can get to the root of your **True Dreams**, passions and desires. These have been placed in your heart by the Infinite One to will and to act according to his good purpose for your life. You must take action and believe in these deep dreams and desires. Trust that God has put them there and will provide the means for them to manifest in your life.

Most people don't go after their True Dreams with passion and persistence. They're either afraid or intimidated. Life just happens or they take it as it comes. Those who choose this route are either passive or reactive — they either passively accept whatever floats their way or react to what happened yesterday or today. This is a classic example of the 80/20 rule — 20 percent of the people produce 80 percent of the results and get 80 percent of the rewards. The other 80 percent of the people struggle for the 20 percent left over, living in scarcity and lack, barely getting by. You don't have to live this way! I'm telling you right now, *you can decide on the direction of your life and set the course of your destiny with intention and purpose*. Decide now to be a part of the 20 percent who go after what they want in life, and put the Power of God to work for *you!*

> *This is the confidence that we have in approaching God: that if we ask anything according to his will, he hears us. And if we know that he hears us — whatever we ask — we know that we have what we asked of him.*[89]

Be *PROACTIVE* and make it happen. Trust that you have your strong God-intended desires for a reason. They were placed on your heart for a greater purpose. Ask according to the will of your Heavenly Father, knowing that he hears you and knowing that you have received it, even as you are asking. Often your prayers are answered before you're even finished praying. Be intentional in your prayers. Be specific and pray with expectancy. These are actions of Faith that please God.

The Law of Attraction's Fatal Flaw

There is a great deal of hype and content currently out on the Law of Attraction. Let me address what I believe to be the fatal flaw in much of what's published on this concept. Most published "Law of Attraction" material attributes a great magical power to "the Universe," suggesting that if you put your requests out to "the Universe" they will return to you fulfilled or even multiplied. The Universe is a vast expanse of matter and mostly empty space. It is a created thing. It has no power, no intelligence and no ability to fulfill your wishes.

Now, to the extent that these commentators are afraid to call "The Universe" God, or are trying to gloss over the concept of God in some politically correct way, so be it. To the others who refuse to believe in or acknowledge God as the all-powerful, omnipotent, omniscient and omnipresent spiritual being that he is, I say — your day will come. I recognize that the prevailing view in the scientific community denies the existence of God (no disrespect intended for the millions of scientists who recognize and honor him). However, Quantum Physics grows closer each day to proving the existence of God and the evidence of Intelligent Design, not only at the macro-universal level, but at the micro-subatomic level as well.

> *"As long as you live merely in the physical and intellectual, you set limitations on yourself that will hold you down as long as you live. When, however, you come into the realization of your oneness with the Infinite Life and Power and open yourself so that it may work through you, will you find that you have entered upon an entirely new phase of life, and that an ever increasing power will be yours. Then it will be true that*

your strength will be as the strength of ten because your heart is pure. O God, I am one forever with you by the glory of a new birth. The celestial powers proclaim it to the utmost bounds of the earth.[90] — Ralph Waldo Trine

I am here to tell you that God is the Creator of all that is known to us (and probably far more that is unknown to us), he is the master of the universe and his dominion is over all, through all and in all. As previously stated, he defies description in our language, because he is beyond our language. He is beyond "he."

So if you're going to put something out in the form of a request, prayer or question, don't direct it to a vacuous expanse of space, direct it to Almighty God, who can actually do something about it! God loves you, wants a relationship with you and wants to bless you.

"How much more will your Heavenly Father give good gifts to those who ask him?"[91]

God answers prayer. God responds to faith. He is pleased to bless your life. He *is* the "Law of Attraction." He established natural law, the laws of thermal dynamics and quantum mechanics. Talk with him. Put your prayers and requests out to him with expectancy and faith. Confidently affirm your relationship with him. Remember the fateful words of Jesus:

"Have faith in God. I tell you the truth, if anyone does not doubt but believes that what he says will happen, it will be done for him. I tell you, whatever you ask for in prayer, believe that you have received it, and it will be yours."[92]

Now *that* is the Law of Attraction right there! *Believe that you have received it, and it will be yours.* With man this is impossible. With "the Universe" this is impossible. Not with God. With the Power of God all things are possible — *all things!*

Recently I helped my friend **Natalie Woodward** manifest her dream husband and her dream teaching job in her dream state (Colorado) within five months on our program. The teaching job in Colorado came very fast — within three months of me facilitating her DTQ. In the last couple months of her teaching Masters degree training, with no teaching experience, in the midst of the 2009 recession, Natalie was offered her ideal teaching job on the spot, in the exact location, exact school district and teaching the exact grade level she wanted! Plus, this happened in a place where jobs are *decreasing* not increasing!

Even though she was very grateful for these two miracles, she desperately wanted to find her soul mate — this was her biggest dream. I encouraged her to pray on her knees for God to prepare her quickly to become the wife he wanted her to be. Natalie memorized Psalms 37:4 and did her best to live it out — "Delight yourself in the Lord and he will give you the desires of your heart." Within two weeks she met her soul mate. It just so happened that he lives in Denver — exactly where she wanted to be! WOW!!! They plan to marry this fall in her dream location, up in the beautiful Rocky Mountains of Colorado!

Did I do this? No way! God did it! I encouraged, coached and helped, but God is the one who did it through Natalie's faith! She took action, put her faith to work and God answered her prayers! Miracles *will* happen when you **ask, believe** and **take action!** Your Heavenly Father wants to do similar things for you.

Natalie learned how to manifest her dreams through the Dream Program and now she's achieving them one after the other. Give a girl a fish and she'll eat for a day. Teach a girl to fish and she'll eat for a lifetime. If you will simply do what I prescribe in this method, you will learn how to manifest your dreams for the rest of your life!

Perseverance and Faith

So often the distance between failure and success is the width of one word — discouragement. This is the devil's most valuable tool, because it is considered harmless by most, which makes it even more insidious and sinister. This small chasm between success and failure is easily bridged by perseverance and faith.[93] Perseverance and faith *crush* discouragement, defeating it completely.

When we fret and worry about things, we are falling into discouragement's trap. At these moments (which we *all* have), we are forgetting God's promises. He is the ultimate Provider. We are reminded of this in a short story Jesus tells:

> *"I tell you, do not worry about your life, what you will eat or what you will drink; or about your body, what you will wear. Is not life more important than food, and the body more important than clothes? Look at the birds of the air; they do not sow or reap or store away in barns, and yet your heavenly Father feeds them. Are you not much more valuable than they? Who of you by worrying can add a single hour to his life?*

> *"And why do you worry about clothes? See how the lilies of the field grow. They do not labor or spin. Yet I tell you that*

not even Solomon in all his splendor was dressed like one of these. If that is how God clothes the grass of the field, which is here today and tomorrow is thrown into the fire, will he not much more clothe you, O you of little faith? So do not worry, saying, 'What shall we eat?' or 'What shall we drink?' or 'What shall we wear?' For the pagans run after all these things, and your heavenly Father knows that you need them. But seek first his kingdom and his righteousness, and all these things will be given to you as well. Therefore do not worry about tomorrow, for tomorrow will worry about itself. Each day has enough trouble of its own."[94]

He promises to take care of our needs. Notice the word "given." God will **give** us what we need — food, clothing, shelter and more. He'll decide how, but the promise remains if we seek his kingdom and his righteousness first, which is only for our benefit. Worry is actually a sign of "little faith" — which is not a place we want to be. Can we trust him? Yes. Can we take him at his Word? Yes. If you follow his direction, your heavenly Father will take excellent care of you.

Gratitude Appreciated

God wants to bless you and make your plans succeed. Why? Because he *adores* you and wants you, his precious child, to be **happy**. He promises to give you the desires of your heart when you delight in him (which means to find your joy in him). He wants a loving two-way relationship with you.

> *Delight yourself in the LORD and he will give you the desires of your heart.*[95]

Don't love him just for the benefits. He knows your thoughts and the motives of your heart. If you are selfishly focused or self-serving, he'll see right through it. On the other hand, if you draw near to him with a sincere heart God will bless your life abundantly, because he loves you and wants to provide for you.

We should be grateful when he answers our prayers. God appreciates our gratitude. He doesn't necessarily "need" it, but in the same way we want our children, spouse or significant other to be grateful when we give to them, God wants us to remember him after he blesses us in our lives. This is important in any two-way relationship.

Take time to notice how he provides for you. Remember to give thanks and be grateful for what you have been *given*. Life will be much more joyful if you maintain this perspective.

Unlimited Power

The beautiful truth is that we have unlimited power and resources available to us through the Power of God! This is the greatest Power. It is the ultimate gift. Nothing surpasses it. We have the Universal Mind of Infinite Intelligence behind us! There is no position too difficult, no problem too hard and no obstacle too challenging that it cannot be overcome with the Power of God. *Nothing* is impossible with him.

When we doubt, fall into worry or discouragement, we chain ourselves down with limiting beliefs. These chains exist *only in our minds!* We have only to believe and the chains will fall away. Faith obliterates doubt and worry. Perseverance defeats discouragement. When we are tempted to shrink back, we must remember these words: "It is the Father living in me, doing his work." The Power of God is *within* us and works through our faith.

When we know God's Power is with us, we can have full confidence. Our decisions can be based on the knowledge of his unlimited resources. We can take initiative with courage, faith and trust in his mighty strength. This truth is what called Abraham out to a new land, led Moses and Joshua, made David invincible and enabled Jesus to perform great miracles. We can choose to put his Power to work in our lives or not. Unlimited power is available to us. The choice is yours.

Practical: Make a list of dreams that could only happen by the Power of God (or your Higher Power). Pray through this list or meditate on them. List them on your Key Cards™. Close your eyes and visualize them. Commit them to the Infinite One and allow his power to work in your life. Watch for what God does in your life to show his love and response to you. Also, pay attention to the promptings of his Spirit, which may give you thoughts, ideas and direction regarding the way you should go.

Reality TV Bite: During the show I was asked to do an impromptu "Dream Workshop" at the soup kitchen in Indiana. The staff from the church that sponsors the soup kitchen was *great* to work with! At the end of the workshop I *gave away* approximately 25 Dream Program Kits I had on hand. The book (the one you're holding) was not yet ready and a few of the attendees asked me about the price of the book and kit I was giving away. Of course, I answered their questions. Unfortunately, the show's editors manipulated the scene to make it look like I was trying to *sell* my kits to the homeless and unemployed people at the soup kitchen that night. This defies common sense! I would *never* do such a thing and did not do it that night. On my website (DreamProgram.com) you'll see quotes from both the associate pastor and pastor's wife of God's Kitchen (the church) who were in attendance that night. They verify the fact that I *gave* the kits away and wasn't trying to sell anything to anyone. How unfortunate that Wife Swap chose to twist their portrayal of the event like this. But God turned it into a victory! The night the show aired, we received the following message from someone who was in the audience at the soup kitchen that night:

"I was homeless... but took the few techniques that I saw you share with the poor people on Wife Swap. I trimmed my hair, started the affirmations and manifested a better situation. I am trying now to get working... Thanks for helping me. I love you. I am such a better person now. Thanks Mark and Dina." -Keith W- May 7, 2010

WOW! It just goes to show that if you take the first steps of action in faith, God can work wonders!

Remember: If you feel you need personal mentoring, coaching and guidance through these or any exercises that are part of the Dream Program visit www.DreamProgram.com/store.

IMPORTANT: Please share your **success stories** and experiences with us so that it may inspire and encourage others. We *can't wait* to hear about the **amazing victories** in your life as you put The 7 Keys™ to work. Contact us at www.DreamProgram.com/contact and share your *Great News* with us!

Part III

Choice & Destination

Dream to Destiny[96]

We all have a destiny
It's part of God's plan
You can fulfill yours
I know you can

It takes courage to follow
His plan for your life
But he'll give you the strength
And make you take flight

It starts with one step
You'll go further each time
Inside each of us
Is a rich goldmine

Follow through now
Go after your dreams
You'll find out
It's not as hard as it seems

Follow your dreams
And bring them to be
When you give them life
You become truly free

By Rob Kenney

Chapter 9

Your Destiny

If you keep thinking what you've always thought
You'll keep getting what you've always got

If you change your mind and start today
You'll take your Life a brand new way

Popular culture asks this timeless but confused question: "Do I have a destiny, or is it all free will?" People are looking for answers. "Is my destiny predetermined by fate, decided by God, or do I determine the outcomes in my life?" These are some of life's most profound questions. We look to others for direction. Most of the time we look everywhere else for answers except inside ourselves.

Imagine your body as a vehicle. You are in the driver's seat of your life. Your **dreams** and **passions** are the fuel for your engine. Your **mind** sets your course and your thoughts are your roadmap. Your **gifts** and **talents** are the wheels that carry you forward, and **God** is the engine that makes it all go. The *combustion* that happens with the air, the spark and the fuel, which fires the engine to make it go, is *all* from God.

- God is the "Engine" providing "combustion" => air/spark/fire
- Passion is the "Fuel" in your tank
- Mind provides your Course "Map" and Thoughts are your "Directions"
- Gifts & Talents are the "Wheels" which get you where you want to go
- You are the Driver, determining the course of your Destiny
- Faith/Belief are the "Turbo Charger" or "Fuel Injection" for your Engine

Now think about your *destination*, your place of arrival. You have the freedom to choose your course. Your thoughts can take you anywhere you want to go, so your destination depends on your choices. It's a function of your faith and it starts with *you!* You must believe. It is not too hard for us or beyond us. In fact, it is very near us.

> This is not too difficult for you or beyond your reach. It is not up in heaven, so that you have to ask, "Who will ascend into heaven to get it and proclaim it to us..?" Nor is it beyond the sea, so that you have to ask, "Who will cross the sea to get it and proclaim it to us..?" No, the word is very near you; it is in your mouth and in your heart... I set before you today life and prosperity...[97]

Not only is it near us, the very Kingdom of Heaven is *within us*.[98] Our destiny is in our hands. Life and prosperity are very near us, not far away. What will we do with it? It is fully within our power to decide. God has given us that power, he has given us the choice and he has planted greatness within us. What we do with all this is our responsibility.

You may say, "What about God? Doesn't his will prevail?" Of course it does. But it doesn't work the way many of us think. God did not make us as robots, to be wound up or programmed to go about our lives in some mechanical predetermined way. He gave us the freedom to choose. He equipped us, endowed us and prepared us for many great things. It is up to us to go out and do them. We have the raw talent and abilities, and we are responsible for developing those and making the most of them.

The greatest secret is the understanding that we can achieve as much as we believe is possible. *Believe you have already received it and it will be yours.* That is faith! It starts with us. God will encourage, support and help us — he is always with us. He'll inspire ideas, give us hunches, guide our "gut," open doors and so much more. He will allow the biggest dreams you truly believe are possible to come true.

Free Will

Destiny is not some elusive thing that happens outside of our control or involvement. "Free will," of course, is our ability to choose. You have a choice in your destiny. It is not determined beyond you. It lies completely within the realm of your decisions and the power to direct the outcomes in your life. Through your mind, you choose the course. Thoughts are your road map. There are many potential outcomes. We can determine — even design — our destiny with purpose and intent, especially with the Power of God behind us.

The most exciting truth is that anything is possible for you! You are the master of your fate. What do you feel driven to do? What are you passionate about? Pursue it! You have **everything** to do with determining the course of your destiny by the decisions you make. Your thoughts, beliefs and actions will determine the outcomes in your life. The ability to *choose* is the most powerful freedom you have.

You are the master of your fate.

The predominant thoughts that occupy your mind will determine the results that manifest in your life. Direct your thoughts positively and positive results will occur. Direct them negatively and negative results will occur. Your thoughts are completely within the realm of your control and you are entirely responsible for them. They will go in the direction you send them.

Your dreams can become your destiny, your reality. You are the catalyst that sets your dreams in motion. You can either choose to control your world or your world will control you. Here again, it's up to you. Everything begins with your thoughts. Thought gives birth to desire. Desire manifests itself into action. Action, repeated over and over, becomes habit. Our habits form our character. Character shapes our destiny. It all begins with a single thought. As we learn to direct our thoughts, we begin to direct our destiny.

The freedom in this message is the power to choose. The liberty we have provides the ability to go and do virtually anything we choose. Consider how amazing this is!

Along with it though, comes the responsibility for our actions and outcomes. Where we end up in our lives is a function of the choices we've made and the actions we've taken. If we have problems, it is not anyone else's fault. We need to drop the victim mentality and take responsibility for ourselves and our actions. If you're in a tough place in your life right now, regardless of the circumstances, you can pick yourself up, decide to make changes and begin new directions *today.* Whatever excuses get in the way (there are usually many) clear them from the table and begin plotting a new course of action. Your life can change radically in a *short* period of time if you will simply decide to change and take action. Don't let excuses or self-justification get in the way. Do yourself a favor, be honest and tell yourself the truth! Then own it and move on. Don't dwell on it or wallow in it like a pig in the mud. Get over it and get beyond it!

Far too often, people sit on the couch, look up to heaven and say, "O God, please help me! Please do something for me!" or "O God, please make me great!" Then they sit there and wait for something to happen. Christians are the worst offenders. They're waiting for

God to do something while they sit on the couch. Then they wonder why nothing happens.

In the meantime, God looks down upon us knowing, "I *made* you for greatness. I gave you many gifts. I've planted passions within you — so *get up, go out and do something with all I've given you!* And remember, **I am with you.**" Nothing happens if we continue sitting on the couch. We must act. We must have the faith, boldness and courage to pursue the dreams and passions within us. If we don't act it's not God's fault, it's *our fault.* God says, "I've given you all these. What will you do with them?" If we squander and waste them, shame on us — we will lose them. If we invest and make the most of what we've been given, we'll thrive and prosper — plus we'll be given more.

Invest Your "Talents"

Take for example the famous Parable of the Talents.[99] In it several servants (employees in today's world) are entrusted with their master's assets and instructed to "put this money to work" while the master is away. Upon his return he calls them in to account. The first servant did well with the five "talents"[100] he was given. He had earned five more. The master praises him, saying *"Well done, good and faithful servant. Because you were faithful with a few things, I will put you in charge of many things. Come and share your master's happiness!"* The second servant also did well, his two talents had earned two more. The master's reply was the same, *"Come and share your master's happiness!"* When the third servant steps forward, he admits to burying the talent in the ground because he was *afraid.* He returns it as it was left to him. He didn't lose it, but he gained nothing from it. The master's reply?

> *"You wicked, lazy servant! ...you should have put my money on deposit with the bankers, so that when I returned I would have received it back with interest. Take the talent from him and give it to the one who has ten talents. For everyone who has will be given more and he will have an abundance. Whoever does not have, even what he has will be taken from him."*

Wow. Very serious! What's the moral of the story? It is not a small matter to squander the gifts and "talents" we've been given. We are called to use them. If we *don't* use what we've been given, we'll *lose* what we've been given — it will either be taken from us or will atrophy from lack of use. We must make the most of what we have, fully investing our talents for the greatest possible return or benefit.

If we don't, we are being *"wicked"* and *"lazy."* I don't want this label, do you?

> *If we don't use what we've been given, we'll lose what we've been given.*

Jesus is telling us to do our best with what we've been **given**. This applies directly to us as far as our gifts and talents are concerned. We have a responsibility to fully utilize them. Only if we are faithful with the "few" things, will we be put in charge of "many" things. Doesn't this make sense? He has the power to multiply our resources and give us abundance or lack depending upon how responsible we are. We have the power to choose to be responsible or not. Decide to cultivate all the "talents" you've been given. When you put your resources to work, opportunities will unfold around you. Don't look for opportunity in the distance, search for it right where you are. There is an abundance of opportunity around you. He has created almost infinite possibilities for your life. Open your spiritual eyes and you will see.

Passion for Greatness

Each of us is a miraculous creation capable of greatness. Not a greatness to serve ourselves, but greatness that benefits our fellow man and the common good. We are all passionate about something, perhaps many things.

These passions are within us for a reason. We must trust that the healthy passions within us are there by design. They serve as fuel for our engines! What are you so passionate about that you would be willing to die for it? When you identify your God-intended passions, you will have very strong clues toward your unique purpose. When we operate within our passions we find our maximum potential, or "highest and best use." Working or living in our highest and best use is where we were designed or created to be. Greatness is easy for us when we are driven by passion to reach our maximum potential.

> *When we operate within our passions we find our "highest and best use."*

The spirit within you is your greatness, your creative genius. Through your spirit and your subconscious mind you connect to the Infinite One and Universal Mind. This is the source of all knowledge and abundance. All things are available to you. All things are possible because God is not limited by time, space or anything else. Your ability to build income and wealth come through this infinite supply chain of abundance. You are surrounded by opportunities.

You are filled with ideas. Free your imagination and your subconscious mind to dream. You are only limited by the boundaries of your beliefs and what you consider possible.

Go in the direction of your dreams by focusing your mind on what you want. Go in the strength that God provides when you use your gifts and talents to build others up. Feed your mind positive thoughts. Read positive, uplifting books. Watch inspirational movies. Fill yourself up with love, gratitude and what is excellent and praiseworthy. Remember the work of Dr. Emoto and the effect that words and thoughts had on water. It is reasonable to believe they have similar effect on us.

Free your imagination and your subconscious mind to dream. You are only limited by the boundaries of your beliefs and what you consider possible.

Think of your inner self as an eagle. In your life, are you functioning at your maximum potential, your highest and best use? Are you being all that you are capable of? What have you been functioning as — an eagle, a sparrow or a chicken? You were created for greatness — go for your inner eagle! Throw off everything that hinders you and step into who you were designed to be. "Free Range" the chicken within you, sing like the sparrow and soar like the eagle.

Cultivate your healthy passions and pursue them with confident faith so that they begin to manifest. It will only happen if you take the first step in faith. Your passions and dreams lead to your unique purpose, your niche in life. You will achieve your greatness if you pursue them.

Power Shortage

You can manifest your dreams and bring them into reality through the power of God or try it on your own power. This too is your choice. It must be said that many have used some of the principles mentioned here without acknowledging or relying on the power of God and seen success. It is possible. However, I don't recommend that.

Doing things solely on your own power is a long, hard task. It would be like trying to work during a power shortage or having a six-cylinder engine that was running on only four cylinders. You might get there, but it will be tough going!

With God *anything* is possible. He is unlimited by time and space. What could take five to ten years without him could happen in a matter of five to ten months with him. Tapping into The 3 Powers™

simultaneously is how God will manifest your dreams faster than would be possible otherwise. I urge you to choose your destiny based on your dreams and passions, gifts and talents. If you place limits on what God will do or allow for you in your mind, you limit your own possibilities.

To become all we are capable of is our ultimate destiny.

If you attempt to reach your destination without God, you can, but you may be in for a long, hard road. I've seen it happen to people over and over again. By the time they reach their destination they're old, tired and burnt out because they did it on their own power. You can try it that way (although you probably wouldn't be reading this book if you were intent on that course) or you can try it my way. Give The 7 Keys™ four months of devoted, faithful effort and see what happens. I believe miracles will happen in your life if you do. You have everything to gain and nothing to lose.

Infinite Wisdom is near you waiting for you to choose him. He wants you to consult with him and his Spirit will guide you. He can empower you to your destination of choice when you ask him, believe and take action. When you ask it demonstrates faith in him. He won't perform miracles when there is a lack of faith. If you are true to yourself, you'll go after your dreams using your natural resources — your mind, gifts and passions. But you are the only one who can make that decision. No one can force you, and God *won't* force you. It is completely your choice.

Once you've discovered your true dreams and gifts through our DTQ™, focus your thought energy on your desired destination. You are the only one with the power to direct your thoughts to be in alignment with your dreams. The only thing you truly control is your thinking. (Your thoughts then control your actions.) So it is completely your choice to go after your dreams. If you go forward in the strength the All-power provides, persistently asking him to manifest your dreams, he will lead you to your desired destination (your dream). If you choose not to, then repsonsibility for any power shortage falls squarely at your feet.

Finding Your Niche

Remember The 3 Circles™ diagram shown before. This tool helps identify the convergence of your Gifts/Talents, Passions/Dreams and the Economic Opportunities surrounding you. If you haven't yet worked through this exercise, please make time to do it now.

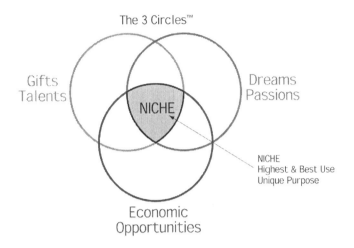

The 3 Circles™

Gifts
Talents

Dreams
Passions

NICHE

NICHE
Highest & Best Use
Unique Purpose

Economic
Opportunities

Discipline your mind and actions to live your life within The 3 Circles. Learn to say "No" to all opportunities that are outside your three circles.

The intersection of The 3 Circles forms the shape of a shield. Your greatness — your niche — is the intersection of The 3 Circles (your "Shield"). Your niche is your unique purpose in life, your highest and best use.

"Shield"

NICHE
Highest & Best Use
Unique
Purpose

Recession-Proof
Shield

Convergence of Opportunity
and Natural Resources

Your niche also represents what I believe to be your "recession proof shield." It is your personal goldmine which will lead you to prosperity, abundance and personal greatness. Stay focused on remaining within your niche. When you have the discipline to stay within your unique purpose, you will be functioning within your highest and best use. This is how you will become the best in your world at what you do. You just may be able to work half the amount of time and achieve double or quadruple the results.

When you diligently go after your dreams using your natural resources and have the power of the Infinite One with you, you can go from dream to destiny. Remember, *you* are the catalyst who gets everything moving. If you don't take action you don't go anywhere. If you don't learn to say "No" to diversions that take you out of your niche, it will take longer to arrive at your dream destination. The result will be lack of fulfillment and unhappiness.

Remember in the parable above, one servant had five talents, another had only two, but the master was equally pleased with both. The important thing is to use what you've been given to its full potential. Be a "good and faithful servant" by putting to use all that you've been given. The master will be pleased with you and *he will* multiply your returns. Not only will he give you more, but he'll invite you to *"come and share [in his] happiness."*

The question we should be asking is: ***What choices should I make to direct my destiny, fully using the gifts and talents I possess?***

The Goldmine Within

There is a rich goldmine that already exists within you. You must learn to tap into it and draw out the rich abundance inside yourself. The goldmine within consists of your gifts and talents, dreams and passions. Your goldmine also includes the ideas given to you from the Infinite Mind. Remember that God has plans for you, to bless and prosper you, to give you a hope and a future.

Your thoughts can be your best ally or your worst enemy. They can be great golden nuggets or arsenic that poisons your water. Take control of your thoughts and learn to use them as a tool to direct the outcomes of your life. When you gain this most valuable skill and discipline, you can become who you were designed to be. You can step into your divine destiny.

Finding your niche (as shown above in the "shield" diagram) and learning to function in it is another rich vein of gold you possess. You will find happiness, true joy and inner peace. Isn't this what we all want?

You can have, do and be anything you want!

You can have, do and be anything you want. This is the golden truth that we must comprehend and embrace. Thankfully this is what my mom frequently repeated and taught me as a child. I believed it then

113

and I believe it now. That's exactly what Jesus meant by having a childlike heart and faith.[101] Because I believed this it became my reality. Let go of your limiting beliefs and remind yourself of this truth regularly, with simple, innocent childlike faith. This is pure gold.

Be Proactive

Many people end up passively taking what life hands them. No one really sets out this way, it just happens. If life does not hand them their dreams, they settle for whatever comes their way. Unfortunately this is why so many feel stuck in life wondering, "How did I get here?"

If you do not think for yourself, the world will think for you. If you do not direct your thoughts, the world will direct them for you. If you do not direct the course of your life, the world will direct it for you. You must take charge! Great freedom and power have been placed in your hands, but if you do not use it, you will never benefit from it. God has given you the complete ability to think, work and act in *any* direction you choose.

If you let the world or others do your thinking for you, you become subject to them. You give up control and allow yourself to be controlled by these other forces. In this way, you let yourself be *blown and tossed by the wind* of popular culture, the media or the opinions of others.[102] This is how we end up in destinations we never planned, anticipated or intended. Sometimes this works out, but not often. Most of the time a passive approach to these matters leads to a life of compromise or mediocrity. It doesn't have to be this way. If you feel stuck in this kind of situation, it doesn't have to *stay* that way. Be proactive. *Don't settle!* Your life can change quickly if you go after your dreams with all your heart (desires), mind (thoughts), soul (prayer) and strength (passion). Persist. Persevere. God is *with* you. Anything is possible.

Inevitably, when we hear inspiring success stories about people, there's a common element. The successful person shares about being *very* focused on their goal, very determined and working very hard towards it — whether it involves business, sports or anything. Obstacles and challenges are usually mentioned too, because they are always part of any victory. These stories encourage and touch us because we love to hear about how others overcame their trials and rose above challenges. So often, victory comes simply from *not giving up!* Perseverance is always necessary and should be expected. Prepare to persist on your journey and don't give up, then *you* will be an inspiring success story for someone else.

Life rarely hands you your dreams. You must go after them! For example, if you want to get married, don't just settle for a person that's in your path. If you seek a certain type of person, go after what you truly desire as you follow the "Manifesting Instructions" in Appendix B. Write out a wish list of your ideal mate's attributes. Then prioritize your list. Set aside a special time to meditate, visualize and pray for the Almighty to bring the ideal person to you. Ask him to prepare you to be an excellent partner as well. Someone out there wants the same thing and is looking for someone just like you! Doesn't it make sense that he'd be pleased with this kind of faithful request? Try this and see what happens. What do you have to lose?

Natalie took this challenge and three of her big dreams became reality within five months. She got her dream teaching job in the midst of the recession which just so happened to be in her dream location. Then she met her soulmate. Now they're planning their dream wedding in her dream location — the Colorado Rockie Mountains — in just a few months. Miracles happen when you ask, believe and take action.

Priorities

Put God in the center of your life. Think of God as the biggest rock and your family as medium sized rocks. Your friends and neighbors are small rocks. Your work and hobbies are pebbles. Put the largest rock, God, in the center of your life. Build your life around the God rock. Put all the medium sized rocks that represent your family closest to the God rock. Then put all the small rocks, your friends and neighbors, next to your medium sized rocks. Last, put the pebbles, work and hobbies, next to the small rocks. Strive to always keep these priorities in check. Let your spouse and children know that they are more important than work, for example.

Right Priorities if Married:	Right Priorities if Single:
God	God
Spouse	Children (if you have any)
Children	Family
Family	Friends/Neighbors
Friends/Neighbors	Career
Career	Hobbies
Hobbies	

Notice how we are supposed to put the Infinite One before people, then people before career and hobbies.[103] When we have the right priorities, we will stand firm when the storms of life come. However, if we don't have the right priorities and put our career or children in the place of God, then our lives fall apart when storms hit. This is why the divorce rate in America is over 50 percent. Put the Almighty first! Put him first each day as you go to him for strength and wisdom in the morning. Put him first when you do what is right in his eyes. Put him first by making his priorities your priorities. Put him first in your finances. Build your life around the God rock and you will stand firm through the storms of life.[104]

Ultimate Destiny

Heaven is the greatest gift of all and the ultimate destiny. There is no greater pursuit than to spend eternity with God. We are spiritual beings first and physical beings second. The world and all things physical will pass away and the only thing left will be the eternal destiny of our everlasting souls.

You were created to have an intimate relationship with your Heavenly Father. This is the single greatest opportunity that exists for us in our lives. But this too is something you must choose. The Father already chose you. He wants oneness with you. He created you with the intention of an intimate relationship with him. Therefore, the "ball is in your court," as they say. No one can do it for you. Only you can choose. Seek out this relationship and pursue it.[105] God loves you more than you can know. God is love. He is patient, gentle and merciful with us. He wants to be your BFF (best friend forever). Can you think of anything better than that? I can't.

During our time here on Earth, he calls us to a high standard. Our model is to be conformed to the character of Jesus and imitate his pure love.[106] Through him only are we reconciled to the Father. With man this is impossible. With God all things are possible. Only with the power of God working in our lives can we reach these lofty goals. Everything is possible for those who believe.[107]

Path of Choice

With the power to choose, we have the ability to direct our lives. We can choose one of many courses. Our choices can lead to either positive or self-destructive outcomes. We can build up or tear down. The direction we choose can lead to great contribution, fulfillment and abundance or the exact opposite.

With this power comes great responsibility. We are accountable for the choices we make and the outcomes that result from these choices. Our choices direct the outcomes of our lives. The sum of those outcomes shapes our destiny. Therefore, *we* control our destiny. It doesn't randomly happen to us. We have everything to do with determining its course.

The truth is, it's not destiny versus free will, one or the other — it's both. Our destiny is determined by the choices we make in our lives. We become what we choose. Our dominant thoughts become the dominant influences on our character. Our choices *direct* our destiny. Our choices dictate our destiny.

The answer to the age old question is simple — your choices direct your destiny. *You* have the power over your choices. Therefore, you have everything to do with directing the course of your destiny.

> *You are fully capable of deciding your own destiny. The question you face is: which path will you choose? This is something only you can decide.*

We must look inside of ourselves for answers. We must decide who we are passionate and determined to become. The Infinite One has given us the power of choice. The answers do not lie outside of us or out of our control. Fate is not predetermined. It is not up to others. Our choice, and the actions behind those choices, will determine the course of our destiny.

Which path will you choose? What choices will you make? You have the power to decide. You have the power to determine your destiny.

Practical: Read through the "Manifesting Instructions" now (The 7 Keys™) in Appendix B. As you study each Key, make an action plan to begin each step. When you follow the instuctions, you will be tapping into The 3 Powers simultaneously. It's very important to be diligent and persistent as you follow this method. As you begin to see and experience results, your faith will strengthen and grow. Remember to express gratitude to God as he manifests dreams in your life.

IMPORTANT: If The Dream Program pointed you in the right direction, tell everyone you care about to get the book or kit so they may benefit too. Together, as we achieve our dreams, we will make a global impact. The "recession mindset" will disappear quickly when people around the world are applying the Dream Program (Dream to Destiny) method in their lives.

__Reality TV Bite:__ I believe I was sent to the unemployed, poverty-stricken "swap" family in Indiana because they had given up on their dreams, maybe even on life. In their own words they described themselves as "fat, redneck couch potatoes and po' white trailer trash" and they were proud of it. This came straight from their "manual" for the show, which is why I used those terms. I was speaking back to them what they proudly said about themselves. (Normally I would *never* use such terms.) In my view these self descriptions justified continued irresponsibility and lack of drive to improve their lives. I encouraged them to dream again and strive to be their best – it's important to put your best foot forward in life! We can always grow if we are humble enough to listen and learn. I taught them how to break the chains of a poverty mindset and change their lives, just as I had. What they choose to do with this valuable information is their responsibility. You can lead a horse to water, but you can't make them drink. Pointing out how to recognize opportunities around them and utilize their natural resources (dreams, passions, gifts and talents), I showed them how they could create a business. Since jobs in their area were scarce, this was a proactive approach. These principles will work for anyone willing to apply them.

__Remember:__ For mentoring or coaching please visit us online at www.DreamProgram.com/store. Several mentoring packages are available. You are worth it! Your dreams are worth it too.

Chapter 10

Faith Conquers Fear

"The only thing we have to fear is fear itself..." — FDR

All of us stand on the verge of greatness. The mortal enemy of this greatness is F.E.A.R. It tries to intimidate us with conjured up notions of terrible things that *could* or *might* happen. These fears only grow when we feed and water them. If they are ignored and starved they will whither and die. But this truth is only discovered *after* we confront and challenge our fears. If we never do, we never overcome them or learn this vital lesson.

Everyone struggles with fear at some level. Those you think are fearless usually are not. They may cover it up well, but they feel fear just like you. Fear is something we all have to deal with, battle and learn to overcome.

Fear is almost exclusively of the mind. If we would only muster the courage to confront our fears by facing them head on with passion, we could crush them. We would also find out there really wasn't that much to be afraid of after all because our fears are usually exaggerated in our minds. We make them much bigger than they truly are. If we are consumed with fear, *we will actually be attracting it to ourselves*, because how we think is how we become.

Sometimes fear is healthy and serves as a warning signal for danger. A hooded stranger walks toward you on a dark street late at night. No one else is around. Your instinct tells you to duck into the nearby tavern for the safety a public place brings. It's wise to obey those fear instincts.

On the other hand, let's say that you love to run. Out of the blue you are invited to run in the Boston Marathon — the biggest distance race in the country. You've never run a marathon before, but now a fantastic opportunity is right in front of you. Suddenly you're gripped with fear. Questions race through your mind. "What if I come in last? What if I get injured? What if I can't finish? What if I *fail miserably?!*" Before you know it, you've talked yourself right out of the opportunity.

This "what if" pattern is a trap we can easily fall into. I say, enter the race. Train vigorously — mentally, physically and spiritually. Follow the "Manifesting Instructions" (Appendix B). Prepare your mind and body for the experience and for success. Conquer this kind of unhealthy fear with practice and preparation.

Self-Sabotage

The truth is, most of us are very skilled at self-sabotage. I'm not sure whether it comes naturally or if it's something we learn to do. We all have insecurities and lack confidence in many areas, but self-sabotage is a common cycle we must learn to identify and eliminate. Our internal insecurity is where self-sabotage begins. We become very good at trapping ourselves into downward-thinking spirals. They usually go something like this:

- If I tried *that,* it might not work or I might *fail…*
- If I *failed*, I might look really *foolish…*
- If I *look* foolish, they'll think I really *am* foolish…
- If they think I'm *foolish*, they won't *like* me…
- If they don't *like* me, I won't have any *friends…*
- Having no friends would be terrible, so I better not *try* that.

We think like second graders and before we take the first step, we've talked ourselves out of it. Internally, we think we're protecting ourselves, but it's really a form of self-sabotage. If we're unaware of this, it becomes a habit — or dangerous cycle — that shapes our character, thus shaping our destiny. Because of fear, most people rarely attempt to go outside of their comfort zones. They live their lives within "safe" boundaries, never going after their true dreams or passions. If we allow our fears to conquer our ambitions, we lose our sense of confidence. Very quickly this can engrain patterns of safe behaviors or decisions and before we know it, we've allowed our fears to rule us. They are often left wondering what "might have been?" These are the seeds of regret.

We think we're protecting ourselves, but it's really a form of self-sabotage.

If we are true to ourselves, we will go after what we passionately long for. In this way we must learn to trust the instincts of our hearts. If we shrink back from opportunities that call us to overcome our fears, our character will suffer. At times like this we need to remember that *we are more than conquerors* and that *if God is for us, who can be against us?*[108] When we are tempted to give into unhealthy fears this thought will encourage us to confront these fears with boldness and courage.

If we know there's a source of strength that is with us, it becomes so much easier to fight our fears. We can rest assured in the knowledge that a higher force supports and strengthens us. For me this is Almighty God, Creator of the universe! There was a time in my life that I had to make a choice to either believe this as fact or throw it out as fiction. Faith is a decision. Because of all the evidence I saw around me, I decided to believe this as fact. In my view, science is stubborn and slow to embrace the truth of the existence of God, but the case builds nonetheless. Here's a sampling of just some of the scientific evidence supporting God's existence:

Evidence — The Faith Decision

1. "The universe seems calibrated (designed) for life's existence. If the force of gravity were pushed upward a bit, stars would burn out faster, leaving little time for life to evolve on the planets encircling them... If the relative masses of protons and neutrons were changed by a hair, stars might never be born, since the element of hydrogen they eat wouldn't exist... If (at the moment of creation) some of the basic numbers had been jiggled, matter and energy would never have coagulated into galaxies, stars, planets or any other platforms stable enough for life as we know it." — *Time Magazine*, "What Does Science tell us about God?" December 28, 1992

2. The Second Law of Thermodynamics indicates that the universe is decaying (entropy). It is not eternal. The universe had a beginning and will have an end.

3. Jesus of Nazareth (also known as Yeshua [Hebrew name], Jesus Christ or the Messiah) was a factual historical figure. His death by crucifixion is a recorded historical fact. His post-resurrection "life after death" was witnessed by approximately 500 individuals, many of whom recorded eyewitness accounts of their experiences with him. The firsthand accounts of the "gospel" books of the Bible, and other New Testament writings regarding Jesus are more than 1000 times more historically reliable than the collective writings of Homer, Aristotle, Plato and Socrates. Jesus' life directly fulfilled over 260 prophecies from the Old Testament. The mathematical chances of that happening intentionally or deliberately are 10 to the 152nd power. He was either a liar, a lunatic or who he claimed to be — the Son of God. A great many allowed themselves to be tortured to death as martyrs in standing up for his holy name — something not done for liars, lunatics or apparitions. After reading his account you can come to no other conclusion than that he was who he claimed to be.[109]

Either the Bible is true or it's a hoax. These are just a few small bits of evidence. There are many more (too many for this book). My personal experiences with God and the deep connection I have with the Scriptures cause me to believe that all of it is true. The Bible states that God created the universe and everything in it. He is the all powerful, omniscient and omnipotent master of the universe. Certainly he has the power to manifest your dreams. Whether they involve finding a soul mate, having children, building your dream home, moving to your ideal city, securing the ideal job, building a business, achieving financial freedom, being fit for life or whatever else you may desire, God has the power to make it all happen. All we have to do is persistently ask him with faith and take action. Miracles happen when we ask, believe and take action.

> *"I am leaving you with a gift — peace of mind and heart. So don't be troubled or afraid."[110]— Jesus Christ*

Combating fears with faith has been the story of my life for 24 years as I've persevered and achieved dream after dream. I'm far from perfect, but each conquest makes me better. It will make you better too. There's a terrific feeling of growth and accomplishment when you overcome your fears through faith. I share this with you to inspire and encourage you to *go after your dreams* using your gifts and talents coupled with your God-intended passions. Cultivate these natural resources. They will give you supernatural energy. Think of The Dream Program and me as your personal cheerleaders. The Dream Program's mentor team is here to cheer you on to your own personal greatness, whatever that may be at www.DreamProgram.com.

Quiet Time

Here's exactly how I've been able to conquer my fears over and over again through my relationship with God. Thankfully, I've learned to have "quiet times" with him each morning before I start my day. I choose to begin my day reading his Word and spending time in prayer or meditation. I *need* this time! It fills me with his strength, inspires ideas and prepares me to be my very best for the day. I take very seriously the inspiration, ideas and direction I get during these times because when I do what his Spirit prompts me to do, it *always* goes well for me. Honestly, I attribute most, if not all of my success to these times. This is because God is faithful and never steers us wrong. If you imitate this process, I am confident it will work for you too!

> *You will keep in perfect peace those whose minds are steadfast, because they trust in you.[111]*

This daily quiet time prepares me mentally, emotionally and spiritually for whatever comes my way during the day. Often I literally pray on my knees, with my head bowed down to the King for wisdom and direction throughout my day. Since Jesus, Moses, King

David, Daniel and many other great people in the Bible prayed like this often, I believe it's a great way for you and me to pray too. He promises that if we humble ourselves before him, he will lift us up.[112] Praying on our knees with head bowed down is an *action* that demonstrates humility and submission to him. He raises high the humble and brings low the prideful.

Pray with all your heart, mind, soul and strength. As you pray through your dreams, close your eyes and see them in your mind as reality. Visualizing is a powerful and important exercise that engages your subconscious mind. Feel the joy of achieving your dreams as you fall asleep each night. Do this same visualizing/prayer technique upon waking each morning as well. Throughout each day, see yourself achieving your desired results (your "Dream Necklace" serves as a reminder for this). Keep doing these daily exercises until your dreams manifest. When you diligently follow this process, you will feel confidence, hope and victory in overcoming the obstacles of life. These feelings are brick wall barriers to your fears.

> *Feelings of confidence, hope and victory are brick wall barriers to fear.*

If you practice these exercises as instructed, new realities *will* begin to manifest in your life. You will see and know that it works! You will be filled with confidence, hope and feelings of victory as you begin to realize your dreams. These barriers are almost impossible for fear to penetrate.

Faith is a decision. Decide to trust in God's mighty power to help you, guide you and protect you when you pursue the dreams in your heart. Your healthy desires and passions are there for a reason. He'll enable you to fulfill them if you tap into The 3 Powers™ and your natural resources. We were designed to achieve our God-intended dreams and benefit the common good, making a positive impact on the world around us.

Faith and Action

Most of us think of faith as something we believe in. Others as something we have or possess — "she has really strong faith..." The truth is, faith is not something we have. It is not an intellectual belief, a possession or even a character trait. In its origin "faith" is a *verb*, not a noun, which is different than most of us think. The root word for faith is the Hebrew word "aman" (aleph-mem-nun). It is a verb. It embodies wholehearted confidence in action. So faith is an *action*, something we do versus something we have. Or rather, it is confident belief that is acted upon.

Although most relate "faith" to the spiritual realm, this is not intended as a religious discussion. Faith is not limited to that space. We all exhibit faith in many ways. Examples are all around us. When we drive, we have faith that others on the road will stop if the light is red, go when it's green, stay in their lane, etc. Absent this, there would be chaos. I could cite many examples of things we take for granted each day that require faith to function.

When it comes to personal faith, most measure this by belief. Do you believe strongly enough in something or in yourself to see it manifest in your life? This concept has been greatly abused in religious, especially Christian circles. Beginning with "Seed Faith," ghost-written for Oral Roberts, the "prosperity gospel" movement began in 1950's American evangelical circles. If the right things didn't happen for you, if you weren't prosperous or "successful," it was because you didn't have enough "faith." This is very dangerous and has led to a twisting of the truth. After all, the Pharisees believed such things.

Rather, faith is shown by our lives. By what we do and who we truly are. In his inspired letter to the early disciples, James, leader of the church in Jerusalem and brother of Jesus, said this:

> ...faith by itself, if it is not accompanied by action, is dead...
> I will show you my faith by what I do.[113]

These are strong words. None of us want faith that is *dead.* Our "faith" is shown not in mere words, but in our actions. What we believe must show itself in what we do. If we let our fears rule us, this shows in our behavior. Let us not shrink back into mediocrity by allowing fear to limit our decisions or the pursuits of our lives.

> *Our dreams begin to manifest when our faith overcomes our fears. Miracles happen when we ask, believe and take action. This is how our dreams become reality.*

Seek Wisdom First

Uncertainty and indecision are also symptoms of fear. When I don't know what to do in a situation, I've trained myself to first ask God in prayer and then go to the Bible for answers. One popular expression says the "BIBLE" stands for "Basic Instructions Before Leaving Earth." I have built the discipline of turning to the Father and his Word for guidance before turning to anyone or anything else. Most often I find clear guidance and direction that gives me confidence from the Holy Spirit and the Scriptures. If I am still unclear after doing this, I'll seek advice from a wise and trusted person with expertise on the subject.

When I'm struggling with a certain emotion or fear, I will typically study that subject out (through a concordance or life-application resource) in the Scriptures to obtain guidance from the Spirit and God's Infinite Wisdom. Then I'll meditate on those thoughts and pray through them during the day. Inevitably, after going through this process I experience a peace and a calmness that fully equips me for the day.

> The peace of God will guard your hearts and minds in
> Christ Jesus.[114]

If I fail or get too busy to practice this discipline, the opposite happens to me. Anxiety, worry and fear grip my mind and heart, resulting in an absence of peace. I've learned to make this a priority because this habit sets me up for success. It enables me to conquer fear with my faith. It will do the same for you.

Thoughts Create Reality

Your thoughts are the energy that drives the "wheel" of your destiny, or the destination you arrive at in your life. Your thoughts lead to your choices. Your choices drive your decisions. Your decisions determine your destiny. These all consist of the *thought energy* that turns your "Destiny Wheel™."

The Destiny Wheel flows in a circular manner in both directions and each part influences the other. Your natural resources – gifts and talents, dreams and passions – are the *physical assets* you possess that enable you to reach your destiny. They all work together in perfect symbiotic balance when God is at the center providing strong foundational support. *Something* is at the center of the "wheel" of your life – if it is not God, it's something else. If this center support is not solid, your wheel will be unstable. If the center is weak or unstable, then fear can easily penetrate your thoughts.

Fear is a powerful, passionate emotion. If we give life to our fears, we will not pursue our dreams. This indirectly feeds our fears, allowing them to grow in power in our lives, which then manifests an unfulfilling existence. This can easily become a vicious, self-defeating cycle.

When we focus on our fears our thought energy is channeled in the wrong direction. It actually energizes the very thing we're afraid of and will make it manifest. Our belief system consists of what we fix our minds on. Physical reality is a manifestation of our thought energy, which is a product of our belief system. Negative belief about yourself becomes your reality. Positive belief about yourself also becomes your reality. For example, if we fear poverty, we will struggle financially. When we believe that we are prosperous, we experience abundance. If we fear failure, we are likely to fail. However, if we truly believe we will be victorious and successful, then we will.

"Why are you so afraid? Do you still have no faith?"[115]

A decision is the first step in the direction of cancelling this cycle and turning things around. It begins with attitude, followed by decision, backed up by action. We must first believe and develop an attitude of abundance. This then becomes a firm decision. Our actions are then based on our new belief system. With faith, we must believe that we have direct access to the source of Universal and Infinite Supply. With confidence, we can turn to the All-power for strength. Abundance will become our reality. Our decision then manifests our experience.

Regret comes not from dreams unrealized, but from dreams *never attempted*. Fear is often the culprit that keeps us from pursuing our dreams. If we never take the first step, we'll never know how sweet the victory can be. We are left wondering what might have been. Regret leaves a bitter aftertaste.

On the other hand, if we go after our dreams and our efforts don't succeed, we know we gave it our best shot even if things didn't go as planned. Valuable lessons are learned when we muster the courage to pursue our greatest desires. Our character grows.

Sometimes this experience is more important than the result we intended. "Shoot for the moon and land among the stars" is what I like to say. This phrase encourages me to aim high. Often the place I land is better than what I had in mind to begin with!

Face Your Fears

Imagine a five-year-old girl standing on stage. She's in a school play and the time has come for her to sing her song. She's standing there, looking so cute in her little dress and bows, before an adoring crowd of parents and teachers. But just as her song begins, she becomes paralyzed with fear. She's standing there, staring blankly out at the crowd in front of her, frozen with stage fright. If she would but open her mouth to sing, she'd be rewarded with applause and cheers of encouragement. With the courage to finish, she'd be congratulated afterwards with everyone telling her how beautifully she sang. She'd think, "Wow, I *like* this! I want to do this *again!*" Next time, she might still be nervous and afraid, but it would be much easier for her to overcome that fear with the memories of encouragement and joy afterward. On the other hand, if she continues to stand there frozen, she will eventually be removed from the stage, never knowing this joy or this victory. She might never *attempt* to sing again. Instead of conquering her fear, her fear *grows* and *conquers her*.

This same thing happens to us. We are standing on the stage of life, and we have a decision to make. We can either step up and sing or stand there paralyzed with fear and do *nothing* until we're removed from the stage. We must realize that there is really not that much to be afraid of. If we would but confront our fears and step into the moment, doors of opportunity and reward open to us that are beyond what we even ask or imagine.

A friend of mine was deathly afraid of sharks. He decided to obliterate his fear by challenging himself to dive in a shark tank. In a controlled environment, with a tank full of well-fed sharks, he donned scuba gear and was submerged with the sharks for several minutes. With sharks swimming all around him, he confronted one of his greatest fears. Several minutes later he emerged from the tank victorious! How did this make him feel? Absolutely terrific! He had conquered his fear.

Another friend was terrified of heights. He decided to do that which he feared most and went skydiving. He decided on a "tandem jump" (where you jump attached to a professional instructor) to face his fear head-on. They were to jump from 12,000 feet with a long free fall before opening the parachute. The jump was successful and not nearly as frightening as expected. This experience genuinely helped him overcome his fear of heights. Now he flies commercially with relative ease and is comfortable going to upper floors in high-rise buildings. He's now been set free from the fear that previously crippled him. What an amazing victory!

Fight Fear With Prayer

When I shared my story with you, I mentioned how fearful I was of having another miscarriage, or even worse — a stillborn baby. I shared how I fought this fear by focusing on pictures of a full term pregnant woman and a healthy, happy baby girl every night before falling asleep. By diligently focusing my mind on the desired result, visualizing and praying with all my heart, I believe that I manifested, through the power of God, my healthy, happy daughter Lauren, born full term nine months later. I conquered my fear with faith and prayer. The exercise of focusing my mind on a successful pregnancy along with visualizing the end result in my mind increased my faith in the unseen. This visualization exercise was what I prescribed to myself for the sole purpose of fighting my fears. I knew that if I continued to fear a dreadful result that it would become my reality. When we give into fearful thoughts, we are allowing our minds to focus on negative results that we do not want to attract. We bring about what we think about — good or bad. We manifest what we focus on.

Scripture says *fear has to do with punishment.* When we feel afraid, we should ask ourselves if we're doing something that we shouldn't be doing. Ask yourself, "Am I being a person of integrity and doing what's right?" If so, there is nothing to fear. The solution to a fear problem is to confront it and drive it away by asking God to remove it. Again, scripture says "perfect love drives out fear." God is love — perfect love.[116] Therefore, we should ask *him* to drive out our fear. Persevere, ask, believe and take action confronting your fears. Only then will they flee from you.

Become who you're designed to be; step into your destiny!

I know this only too well, because I have to fight fear with my faith almost daily. The evil one tries to take our minds captive with fear. It is among his strongest weapons. He tells us lies and conjures up exaggerated notions to make us fearful. These hold us back, keeping us from achieving our divine destiny and benefitting the greater good. All of these undesirable results hurt us. When we conquer our fears, we become who we are designed to be. We step into our divine destiny. We *benefit* the greater good. All of these hurt the evil one. This battle is best fought with the weapon of prayer.

Our Message of Hope

The message my husband and I want to bring to everyone is a message of *hope*. In spite of challenging economic times, you can pursue and live your *dreams!* Using your natural resources — gifts, talents, passions and desires — you can rise above circumstances that surround you, regardless of what they are. With the *power available to you* — the power of your *mind*, the power of *passion* (or the *human spirit*) and the *power of God* — *anything is possible!* Nothing is impossible or beyond your reach. Opportunities surround you! Let nothing hold you back, for you have nothing to fear. You have access to unlimited power, resources and intelligence. You are only limited by your faith and what you're able to believe. So *believe BIG*, think *BIG* and *DREAM BIG!*

If you believe — I mean you *believe that you have already received it* — you will receive whatever you ask for in prayer. As you think, so you will become. Your life will be the manifestation of your predominant thoughts. Because your subconscious mind is the link to the Infinite Mind (the Mind of God), you have access to Infinite Intelligence, Infinite Wisdom and Infinite Supply. You have access to his unlimited bounty and power through faith.

"For I know the plans I have for you," declares the LORD,
"plans to prosper you and not to harm you, plans to give you
hope and a future."[117]

Almighty God has plans to bless you with a bright future. He wants to prosper you and give you hope. You do not need to worry. Abundance surrounds you. You abound in all good things. Everything you need to be successful already exists within you — they are your natural resources. If you believe you will receive whatever you ask for in prayer. All things work for your good if you love God — this is a promise. You can do all things through his Infinite Strength. You have nothing to fear, because all things submit to him, and you are in him as he is in you. You have heavenly weapons that cannot be defeated or overcome. With him, you are invincible.

Your gifts, talents, passions and dreams were planted in you for a reason, with an intended purpose and a plan for their use. They are there by design so that you may live a blessed and fulfilling life, benefiting the common good, glorifying God and making the world a better place for you having been in it.

May you be richly blessed! May your Dreams become
Your Destiny!

Practical: List the reasons that connect most directly with you from this chapter why there is really no reason for you to fear. Make the list as long and strong as you like. Post this list or keep it in a handy place so that you may refer to it in times of worry, fear and anxiety. This list will serve to encourage you and help you overcome you fears in these times of struggle.

Make sure to complete your Key Cards™ per the instructions in Appendix D, if you have not done so already. Fill out two identical cards to pray/read through aloud morning and night as directed. The Key Cards are essential in manifesting new realities. If you've gotten new insight or inspiration for your dreams, please feel free to update or revise your Key Cards accordingly. You will want to do this from time to time anyway, as dreams that have manifested are replaced by new dreams. When your Key Card is memorized, pray/read through your dreams as you're falling asleep, visualizing them as your mind goes into the theta brainwave state, engaging the subconscious mind. This process will never stop working.

Reality TV Bite: My husband and I knew going in there was a possibility the show's producers would twist the "reality" and try to make one or both of us look bad. Knowing this, we had to face our fear if we were to do the show. We filmed for 26 total days in both locations for 12-16 hours per day. They end up with over 300 hours of raw content to work with. The editors (people we never met or talked to) then go to work creating the 44 minutes of program that becomes the one-hour episode. They can make the show whatever they want — and they do. Scenes are edited out of context or sequence and twisted to appear as something they are not. They bend the content to fit the show they've planned. Far from reality! I suppose that's why it's said, "There's not much reality in Reality TV!" The most encouraging things happened after the show aired. In spite of the fact that the producers did everything possible to portray us negatively, we were overwhelmed with positive response. We immediately began receiving hundreds of emails, messages and calls from people who loved our message of hope and wanted to know more. We are so grateful! Even though they tried to do us harm, God intended it for our good!

Remember: Share your success stories with us at www.DreamProgram.com so that others may be inspired by your faith and your victories. May God bless you with even more to be grateful for as you go from Dream to Destiny.

**Dream to Destiny**

Appendix A — D

DreamTouch™ Questionnaire

Plan to take about **45 minutes of quiet, uninterrupted time when you are most alert**, to answer these soul searching questions to discover your *TRUE* dreams, gifts and talents. Adjust the atmosphere in your home by playing the Focus DVD that comes in the Dream Program Kit. Select **"nature sounds"** to engage your senses to feel like you're on a secluded island retreat. It is vital to be in a relaxed state where you can concentrate and focus.

A brief time of prayer or meditation is recommended before you begin the DTQ™. If you are a person of prayer, you are encouraged to pray before you begin with something like this: *"Thank you for the many blessings in my life. Thank you for the gifts given to me at birth. I pray for your wisdom to know what they are and then to use them for the greater good. Show me how to reach my full potential and destiny that you have planned for my life."* If you prefer meditation, concentrate on the same thoughts of gratitude, blessings, gifts, wisdom and life direction.

Start the DVD taking **one minute to meditate on nature's beauty.** Clear your mind of all distractions. After reading each question, feel free to close your eyes, searching your heart for the answers. Give yourself about 30-45 seconds to answer each question. Write down the *first* thoughts that come to your mind, unedited. Some questions may seem redundant. This is designed to draw out your true dreams and gifts. (Please record your answers either on this form or separately in your journal or notebook.)

1) List all the people and situations that make you feel extremely happy, putting a big smile on your face and joy in your heart.

2) List all the people and situations that make you laugh heartily.

3) Imagine you just won the $10,000,000 lottery! You never have to work another day in your life…

    a. Where do you choose to live, anywhere in the world?

    b. Who is with you?

    c. What do you enjoy doing in *all* your free time?

    d. Do you choose to work? _____ If so, what would you want to do?

4) Think back when you were 7 to 12 years old…

    a. What did you LOVE to do often?

    b. What did you want to be when you grew up and why?

5) If you can't sleep at night, what do you do? (Read, draw, write, etc. This is your 3 a.m. passion.)

6) The questions below will help you uncover your **TOP 5 GIFTS…**

    a. When you were a child, what did your loved ones tell you that you were a natural at?

b. What does your best friend, spouse or others close to you say that you're gifted at?

c. List ALL the activities that make you feel energized. (You feel filled up rather than depleted.)

d. List your TOP 5 <u>Gifts</u>. (These come so naturally that you may take them for granted.) **See Gift List (Appendix C).**

1. _____   **2.** _____

3. _____   **4.** _____

5. _____

7) What are you passionate about? (You are *highly* enthusiastic about this.)

8) What do you love, love, love?

9) What would you do if you knew, without a doubt, that you would succeed?

10) What could you be the <u>best</u> in the world at, maybe with some training? (best is *your* world or in *the* world)

11) You just died at a ripe old age. Your spirit is hovering far above the people at your funeral. You can see all the attendees...

   a.   Who would you want to be there?

   b.   What do you want them to be saying about you?

12) Take a few minutes to review all of your answers above.

   a.   List all that you are extremely grateful for.

   b.   What do you strongly desire?

   c.   What is your TRUE DREAM? (This statement will later be shared on your Key Cards.)

   d.   Describe the kind of person you want to be in four "I am..." statements. These should support your dream goal.

WARNING: Beware of dream stealers. Choose to share your precious dreams with a select few who will be positive and supportive. Protect your dream like a newborn baby. Believe that your dream(s) can be achieved. Cast off fear by tapping into your Higher Power daily through prayer or meditation. When you draw on the power source greater than your own *no one* will be able to stand up against you! You can be confident, strong and courageous. *"Do not be terrified or discouraged, for the LORD your God will be with you wherever you go." (Joshua 1:9)*

Go confidently in the direction of your dreams. Become who you are meant to be! You have been given gifts and talents, dreams and passions for a reason — to achieve your **unique purpose** in life. This is your **niche**, your **highest and best use**. This is your *Destiny!*

To Begin: Your TRUE DREAM statement and "I am" statements will be transferred onto your Key Cards™ (Appendix D). Please be sure to carefully read the Key Card Instructions *BEFORE* you fill in the blanks. After you thoroughly understand what you're going to do with your cards, fill in the blanks on two of your Key Cards. The answers from the DTQ will help you complete your Key Cards.

Important: If you would like assistance going through this process please go to www.DreamProgram.com/store and sign up for one, several or unlimited mentoring sessions. We are available to help you achieve your dream life.

Share Your Story With Us: When great things happen for you share the news with us at www.DreamProgram.com/contact.

Manifesting Instructions (The 7 Keys™)   Appendix B

Please make sure you have *read the entire book Dream to Destiny before attempting to implement The 7 Keys.* **Before you begin with the Manifesting Instructions, complete the DreamTouch™ Questionnaire (DTQ™)** while watching the **Focus DVD** (which comes with the Dream Program Kit) to discover your true dreams and gifts. If you follow this program diligently, you will uncover your niche in life — **your unique purpose.**

"If it is to be, it's up to ME" is a slogan to think about often. It all begins with you. You are the catalyst who sets your dreams in motion. You must ask, believe and take action. Miracles happen when you ask and believe! Your dreams can become your physical reality when your faith and your actions are combined with a Power source that is above and beyond you. Be attentive to the promptings that occur to you. This is how I've manifested my dreams for more than 24 years.

Belief or faith in a Higher Power is essential. Know that your Higher Power (mine is God) will be with you and show you the way. Faith is a decision — being **sure** of what you *hope for* and **certain** of what you do not currently see. If you have difficulty believing in God, or the existence of a Higher Power, I ask you to decide to believe for six months and see what happens. Test this process. Be attentive to the promptings that may seem to suddenly occur to you. Ask him if he is there and wants to be a part of your life. You may be surprised at what happens. You have nothing to lose and everything to gain.

Decide to have full faith (free of doubt) while you diligently follow all seven of these keys. You will see amazing results because you will be tapping into **The 3 Powers™** (Mind, Passion and God) *simultaneously.* The tri-union of these three incredible energy sources gives you a supernatural ability that transcends both time and space. (Review Part II of the main text — "The 3 Powers" — to refresh your understanding of these.)

Earlier we talked about "Positive Replacement" where you can replace negative thoughts or behaviors with positive equivalents in just three weeks. It only takes 21 days to form a new habit. You can transform any thought or behavior with this method. Create the habit of DOING this practical method and soon it will become second nature to you. Replace any unpleasant thoughts and habits with ALL seven of the healthy exercises listed below in The 7 Keys and watch your dreams manifest. When you do, you will gain the ability to manifest your greatest desires through the Highest Power for the rest of your life.

The 7 Keys to Manifesting Dreams:

Key 1: Discover Your True Dreams by answering the DTQ™ (Appendix A) while watching the Focus DVD that comes in the Dream Program Kit. Select the "Nature Sounds" audio track on the DVD while you focus on nature's beauty for one minute before answering each of the soul-searching questions. This process helps you escape mentally to a secluded island retreat while you answer each question. This assessment is *key* to helping you discover your **true dreams**, your **passions** and your naturally endowed **gifts**. These *natural resources* will lead to your *unique purpose, your niche in life.*

If you hope to manifest your dreams, you must first know what they are. Napoleon Hill taught, "Whatever the mind can conceive and believe it can achieve." This is true!

Tip: Once you uncover your *True Dream* (there may be more than one), hand write a **wish list** of the most important qualities your manifested dream will possess. Then prioritize these traits. For example, if your dream is to be happily married to your life partner then make a list of the qualities that he or she will have. Then close your eyes and visualize what you just wrote down and pray for your Higher Power to bring him or her into your reality quickly. Ask to be prepared mentally, emotionally, physically and financially for your dream spouse's arrival. Request that your new partner will be prepared for you as well. Then go in the direction of your dream, faithfully walking through the doors that will open! Expect to be led directly to your spouse.

Key 2: Take Inventory of Your Unique Gifts Take full inventory of all your gifts NOW. It's important to make a full assessment of ALL your gifts. The DTQ will help you identify many of your gifts. Refer to Chapter 3: Gifts and Talents, for a thorough discussion on this topic, and the Gift List of Appendix C for further help. (There are many good online gift assessments, many of which are free. If you feel the need, use one of these tests to help you in this process. Search "free online gift assessment.") Write them down on the appropriate line of your Key Card now.

The gifts you were endowed with were placed within you for a reason. They were designed for use. They are part of the goldmine within you. When you are using your gifts, you feel energized. You have a supernatural energy. The reverse is also true — if you're working outside of your gifts you'll feel fatigued, frustrated and unhappy. Imagine if everyone chose their professions based on their gifts.

To waste or not utilize your God-given gifts is downright irresponsible. If you don't use them, you will eventually lose them. Decide to use your gifts (natural resources) and put them to work for you. Meditate on how to use them for the greater good. Doing this will bring great joy, fulfillment and satisfaction. Set your mind to utilize your gifts to achieve your dreams.

Key 3: Feed your Subconscious Mind Please refer to your **Key Cards**™ in Appendix D. Your Key Cards are the main tool you'll use to feed your subconscious mind. By consciously giving your subconscious mind positive instructions through affirmative statements, you will be planting and sowing the seeds of your dreams. Twice daily declare these statements, reading them out loud from your Key Cards — first thing in the morning upon waking and at night just before retiring. Your subconscious mind is at work 24/7 giving instructions to your conscious mind, which controls your actions (Chapter 6: The Power of the Mind).

This process will imprint your dreams and desires on your subconscious mind, which is connected to the Universal Mind. In this way you are pre-programming your expected outcomes before the Infinite Power, who has the ability to bring about any outcome. All things are possible for those who believe.

Refer to your DTQ for help in constructing your Key Card statements. These must be powerful, proactive, declarative statements. Be *bold!* Then follow the Key Card instructions *diligently.* Not only will this help you stay focused on your dreams, it will also strengthen your faith and belief. This is what's necessary to ward off fear and doubt. Decide to feed your subconscious mind every morning and evening following the Key Card process and your dream *will manifest!*

Note: Sometimes in my sleep, the Infinite Mind gives me dreams about how to reach my goals. It's like he's giving me the answers to an exam. If you have a particularly vivid dream that seems to be instructing you, immediately write it down in your journal when you wake up so that you don't forget it. Get in tune to receiving answers and ideas in your dreams as well as during your waking hours. Act on them with care.

Key 4: **Visualize Your Dream:** Visualization is a very powerful and effective exercise, and there are several methods that work effectively (Chapter 6: The Power of the Mind). Four methods are recommended: Concentrated Visualization, Memory Trigger Visualization, Picture It and Dream/Vision Boards. For full explanations of these methods, please refer to the *Dream to Destiny* text in Chapter 6.

Concentrated visualization is a quiet, deeply relaxed state of meditative mental focus. Memory Trigger Visualization is any physical reminder of your dream (such as the key pendant included in the Dream Program Kit). "Picture It" visualization literally means to draw a picture of your dream ("dream scenes"). Dream/Vision Boards are typically collages of images that represent the vision of your manifested dreams realized. All of these exercises are powerfully effective methods for visualizing your dreams. Use any or *all* of them.

The **key pendant (included in your Dream Program Kit)** is best worn as a necklace. Your pendant is simply a tool, a physical reminder of your most important dream. Every time you see or feel your key pendant pray, meditate or visualize your dream manifesting. This is a powerful and effective way to train your mind in the directions of your dreams.

Note: When I wore my original dream necklace around the clock, I was praying for a way to help people in the recession. Within two months the Dream Program and this book were born. Within four months a network television producer flew out to my home and began filming us. Over the next few years you will see my husband and I sharing the *Dream to Destiny* message on **national Network TV (ABC) and in 21 countries around the world.** God is able to do "*immeasurably more than all we ask or imagine, according to his power that is at work within us.*"[118] This is a miracle! Incredible opportunities will come your way too. But they only come when you *ask, believe* and *take action.*

Key 5: Train Your Thinking In re-directing the course of your life's destiny, nothing is more important than training your thinking. This is because everything starts with your thinking. Thoughts contain energy, and this energy can be directed positively or negatively, producing either beneficial and constructive results or harmful and destructive results. For this reason, it is essential to train your thinking. Several practical methods are recommended to accomplish this key.

Become practiced at *taking captive negative thoughts and replacing them with positive thoughts*. Recognize the nature and direction of your thoughts. Develop an awareness of them and learn to identify in yourself control of the direction of your thinking. Practice "Positive Replacement" as described in Chapter 6: The Power of the Mind. Choose positive thoughts to replace negatives, filling the void their removal leaves behind and align your thoughts with your dreams.

Build the habit of writing in your **journal or notebook** daily. Writing by hand, record your positive aspirations, thoughts, goals and ambitions. This exercise is especially effective if practiced before falling asleep. Hand written "I am" statements of the deep desires you are manifesting, practiced repeatedly will imprint themselves on your subconscious mind. When you go there in the mind, you'll go there in the body because *as we think, so we become.*

Draw sketches of the dreams you are manifesting ("dream scenes") by hand. Do this often in your journal — it doesn't matter if you're not artistic! This is a powerful practice that trains your thinking.

Handwrite a list of 10-15 people or circumstances you are grateful for each day in our journal. Focusing on gratitude is powerful both mentally and emotionally. This is best practiced at the beginning of your day when your mind is relaxed. This exercise trains both your conscious and subconscious mind. Develop the habit of saying "thank you" to the Almighty (or Higher Power) throughout the day for the blessings that come your way. As a result, you'll feel grateful and joyful all day long. God is pleased with grateful hearts and wants to bestow blessings on your life (similar to the parent child relationship dynamic).

We must train our thinking. Our repetitive thoughts create desires, which lead to actions, that turn into habits, that become character traits, that shape our *destiny.* Thought — Desire — Action — Habit — Character Trait — Destiny.[119] *Control your thoughts; control your destiny!* Only you can train your mind to think about all that is positive and healthy in order to reach your dreams. Our subconscious mind never sleeps. It is always working — either for you or against you. We must learn to win this battle and direct the power of our thoughts for our benefit. This is the *Key!*

Whether we realize it or not, there is a spiritual battle going on for control of our thoughts. The spiritual forces of evil drive negative thoughts into our minds to keep us down and steer us away from our divine destiny. Win the battle for your mind by cancelling *every* negative thought and replacing them with positive and grateful thinking instead. Choosing to think about what is true, right, noble, pure, lovely and excellent will strengthen you.[120] The Infinite Mind tells us to think this way for our benefit.

Key 6: <u>**Tap into your Higher Power**</u> Drawing on a power source greater than our own is essential. The best way to practice this is with **daily prayer and meditation**. It is necessary to be frank in our discussion at this point. My strong belief is in Almighty God as the Highest Power. And while I do not apologize for my beliefs in this way, I understand and respect that not everyone is in the same place. If you struggle in your belief in God, ask him to show himself to you. Acknowledge that there is a higher spiritual power above and beyond you. If even this is a struggle for you, then please give this book to someone who will benefit from it.

Your friendship with God (or Higher Power) is *vital*. Develop a best friendship with him. He loves you so very much. Above all, he desires a *relationship* with you. Read his Word daily — it is his love letter to you. Prayer is a conversation with him. Meditation is an excellent way to be still and listen to his voice. Have two-way communication with him.

Persistently *ASK* him with full faith to lead you to your dreams. It's important to ask him for what you want. *"How much more will your Heavenly Father give good gifts to those who ask him?"*[121] (Don't ask the universe, ask the One who *created* the universe!) Ask, seek and knock.[122]

"According to your faith it will be done for you."[123] Have faith and do not doubt.[124] Believe that you have already received what you are asking for. *Feel it!* Thank him in advance for answering your requests. Follow where he leads you by taking action on the opportunities that arise. If a door closes, look for an open window and faithfully climb through it. Lack of faith is a *sure* way to keep miracles from happening in your life.[125]

The Heavenly Father wants his children to be happy. Our *true dreams* were placed on our hearts for a reason. They lead us to our *divine* destiny. If we were not capable of achieving our dreams, we would not have them in the first place. His faithful promise is to bless us with the desires of our hearts when we find our delight (our joy) in him[126] (Chapter 2: Discover Your True Dreams).

Tap into the Highest Power and watch your dreams manifest. I may plant the seeds, you may water them, but it is God who makes them grow![127]

Key 7: <u>**Surrender**</u> This idea may seem like a paradox at first. *Surrender* to win your dreams? How can that be? We have mentioned throughout the main text and in the Manifesting Instructions that your subconscious mind never sleeps, and that there is a Higher Power beyond you. The Key to Surrender is peace. Sometimes we can hold on too tight or try to force results that are unnatural or unhealthy for us.

There is great peace in letting go and trusting that the right results will manifest. This is no excuse for passivity or complacency. Far too often, these can feed procrastination, which is an arch enemy to your dreams. On the other side are wrong motives, selfish ambition or worse — greed. With grit and determination, you may get what you eventually want, but it will likely come at great cost.

However, when the peace of surrender is present, results naturally manifest. Sometimes they are different than we envisioned — usually better. Doors may close only for better ones to open instead. When you are connected to the Infinite Mind, you will often be led in new directions. Again, these are often better than what we had in mind to begin with. *Trust* this guidance because it comes from a Supreme Source. What changes is *you*. Whether it be an idea, opportunity or direction, trust these promptings.

As you follow the six Keys above, pray or meditate with a surrendered attitude. For example: "According to your will, please lead me to my dreams and my divine destiny. You know my heart and mind. May my dreams match your dreams for my life. Open the doors. Help me see the way that I should go. I pray to trust and surrender." He knows what's best for you and will do even more than you ask or imagine.[128]

Every few months, have a special quiet time ceremony as you feel the need. Hand write a surrender prayer on a piece of white paper and turn this paper into a white **surrender flag** by taping it to a long stick or straw. Raise this flag in the air and vocalize your surrender to the Almighty, trusting that the answers will come. I've learned the hard way that when I have a surrendered heart, not holding on so tightly to what I want, everything works out faster and better in the long run. God is ultimately in control and we certainly don't want to be struggling against him. Surrender is the *key* to peace.

Now — Put it into Practice! Stay focused and diligently put all of The 7 Keys into practice. Never give up on your dreams! Choose to have a surrendered heart in case the Almighty has something better planned for you. Hold on to your visions, passions and dreams. For without dreams, people slowly die.

Ask, pray and meditate for ideas to create your action plan. When you stay closely connected to your dreams, the perfect path will be revealed to you. Choose your thoughts wisely and carefully. Speak encouraging words to yourself and train your mind for successful results.

Note: Our mission is to help you achieve your dreams by way of your natural resources. Our team is dedicated to helping you and available for one-on-one or group mentoring and workshops at www.DreamProgram.com/store. Send your success stories to www.DreamProgram.com/contact. Please refer your friends and family to www.DreamProgram.com so that we may help them as well.

Copyright 2010 The Dream Program, All Rights Reserved. Patent Pending Method[129]

Gift List (Partial)   Appendix C

We each possess a unique set of gifts. It is my belief that these gifts were given to us by God. In identifying your God-given gifts, you find Keys to your "niche" in life – your highest and best use. Your gifts are part of the goldmine within you – your natural resources.

Fully developing your gifts enables you to become the person you are meant to be, stepping into your destiny. When we do what we were created to do, we will excel and become the best in the "world" at what we do. We will also be fulfilled in our pursuits because we will be doing what are designed to do. Typically we are passionate about such things.

You are meant to use your gifts to build up your family, your community and benefit the common good. When you work in the area of your gifts, you are "your Best YOU!" You will love what you do when you do what you love.

The following is a partial list of Gifts. **Circle Your *Top 5 Gifts*:**

Acting/Dramatic Arts	Language
Administration	Leadership
Affection	Listening
Analytical	Mathematics
Artistic/Creative	Music/Musical Performance
Athletics	Optimism
Beauty	Orator/Public Speaking
Business	Organization
Communication	Patience
Compassion/Empathy	Peace/Calm
Confidence	Performing Arts
Cooking/Baking	Persistence
Contributing to Others Needs	Physical Stature/Size
Dance/Movement	Physique/Form
Deduction	Pleasant Disposition
Diligence	Preparedness
Discernment/Judgment	Prophecy/Seer
Encouragement	Self-Disciplined
Entertainment	Serving/Service to Others
Entrepreneur	Showing Mercy
Faith/Belief	Teaching/Instruction
Generosity/Giving	Wisdom
Healing	Written Word
Health	
Hospitality	_____
Humor/Comedy	
Intellect/Intelligence	_____
Joyfulness	
Knowledge	_____

IMPORTANT: Read these instructions thoroughly before you begin filling in your **Key Cards**.

Before you fill in your Key Cards, make sure you complete the DTQ™. A key ingredient for your success is that you know your **TRUE DREAMS** and **GIFTS** as discovered through the DTQ. Two ingredients are essential in manifesting new realities: A **strong desire** for your new reality and **complete faith** that it can be manifested. As you follow the Key Card exercise as taught in this appendix, your faith will increase as it is exercised and strengthened.

Establish the habit of reading or praying through your Key Card *out loud just before laying your head down to sleep each night and immediately upon waking in the morning*. Please hand write your statements in the blanks on one of your Key Cards. After you completely fill in your first Key Card, write the identical information on a second card. Keep one card next to your bed and the second card in your bathroom (or another convenient place where it will be available to you first thing upon waking) — in case you forget or cannot read or pray through the card next to your bed.

Write your dreams as positive, affirmative statements on these cards. This process is one of **The 7 Keys**™ to manifesting your dreams. You will be employing The 3 Powers simultaneously — Mind, Passion and God. After faithfully and persistently reading or praying through these cards, take action on the promptings, thoughts and ideas you receive. This phenomenon occurs at a spiritual level where nothing is too difficult and anything is possible.

The Key Card exercise feeds your subconscious mind at its most receptive times of day, when your brain is in the Alpha and Theta brain wave states as described in Chapter 6: The Power of the Mind. (Television advertisers take full advantage of these brain states for maximum penetration.) As you read or pray through your cards *out loud, twice daily*, not only will you be tapping into **Infinite Intelligence** through the **Infinite Mind**, but you will also access **The 3 Powers**™:

➢ **The Power of the Mind**
➢ **The Power of Passion**
➢ **The Power of God**

This Key Card exercise helps to increase and strengthen your faith. Without faith, miracles cannot and will not happen. Faith in God (or your Higher Power) drives out fear and doubt. Even though fear is the natural response to any change, strengthened faith overcomes fear. When we act in faith, the Almighty is pleased.

[Personal note: I often pray on my knees with my head bowed down to the ground humbly asking God to manifest my strongest desires. I pray with all my heart and mind, closing my eyes and visualizing my dreams being realized. The connection I feel with him during these times is amazing. I suggest that you do the same and experience this same wonderful bond.]

Once your card is memorized, speak or pray through your dreams, visualizing them as you're falling asleep. Feel the joy of your dreams coming about. Do this exact exercise upon waking every morning *until your dream is manifested* (Chapter 6: The Power of the Mind).

Below is my personal Key Card. On the next two pages are four Key Cards for you. (There are two extra cards in case you need to tweak them over the first few weeks.) **Important:** Only choose words that are positive, that you want to manifest. For example, instead of writing "I am debt free" write, "I am financially free." Avoid using negative words such as "debt" in your statements. Instead, use positive words of things that you *want* to manifest.

Remember that "I am" statements are crucial because you will be tapping into the power of the Almighty within you. He is the great "I Am" and his Spirit lives in you. He breathes life into you daily. Another reason to say "I am" is that you can only control yourself and no one else. "I am" is a powerful, positive affirmative. With it you are taking action and responsibility for your life, direction and circumstances.

Dina's Key Card…

Key Card™ (I pray through this card out loud daily before falling asleep & upon waking.)

Thank you for my unique gifts — *encourager, inspirational, faithful, visionary leader, business minded & driven.*

Thank you that I'm passionate about *encouraging people to use their gifts, talents & passions to step into their destiny. Thank you that I am passionate about my husband, children, family, friends, others & "Dream to Destiny."*

I use my gifts, talents & passions for the common good, building up my family & my community.

Dream Goal: **I see myself** *as an excellent wife, mother & friend.* **I see myself** *as an inspirational leader making a positive difference in the lives of many, who is financially free.*

I am *my best, I do my best, I look my best,* **I am *my Best ME!*** **I am** *who I want my children to become.* **I am** *a strong & successful business woman earning over $X/year.* **I am** *an excellent steward of all I am blessed with.* **I am** *giving back generously plus saving for retirement & education.* **I am** *fit for life, 114 pounds, healthy and strong.*

I can do all things through your strength. All things are possible for me when I ask, believe & take action. Please bring these into my reality or change the desires of my heart. Strengthen me to become who I am meant to be and step into my destiny.

Thank you for blessing me abundantly. I love & trust you completely. Amen.

<u>Key Card</u>™ (Read/pray through this card *out loud, twice daily* before falling asleep & upon waking)

Thank you for my unique gifts —

_____.

Thank you that I'm passionate about

_____.

I use my gifts, talents & passions for the common good, building up my family & my community.

Dream Goal: I see myself

_____.

I see myself

_____.

I am

_____.

I am

_____.

I am

_____.

I am

_____.

To God (or your Higher Power): I can do all things through your strength. All things are possible for me when I ask, believe & take action. Please bring these into my reality or change the desires of my heart. Strengthen me to become who I am meant to be and step into my destiny.

I am my Best ME! Thank you for blessing me abundantly. I love & trust you completely.

<u>Key Card</u>™ (Read/pray through this card *out loud, twice daily* before falling asleep & upon waking)

Thank you for my unique gifts —

_____ .

Thank you that I'm passionate about

_____ .

I use my gifts, talents & passions for the common good, building up my family & my community.

Dream Goal: I see myself

_____ .

I see myself

_____ .

I am

_____ .

I am

_____ .

I am

_____ .

I am

_____ .

To God (or your Higher Power): I can do all things through your strength. All things are possible for me when I ask, believe & take action. Please bring these into my reality or change the desires of my heart. Strengthen me to become who I am meant to be and step into my destiny.

I am my Best ME! Thank you for blessing me abundantly. I love & trust you completely.

<u>**Key Card**</u>™ (Read/pray through this card *out loud, twice daily* before falling asleep & upon waking)

Thank you for my unique gifts —

_____.

Thank you that I'm passionate about

_____.

I use my gifts, talents & passions for the common good, building up my family & my community.

Dream Goal: I see myself

_____.

I see myself

_____.

I am

_____.

I am

_____.

I am

_____.

I am

_____.

To God (or Higher Power): I can do all things through your strength. All things are possible for me when I ask, believe & take action. Please bring these into my reality or change the desires of my heart. Strengthen me to become who I am meant to be and step into my destiny.

I am my Best ME! Thank you for blessing me abundantly. I love & trust you completely.

<u>Key Card</u>™ (Read/pray through this card *out loud, twice daily* before falling asleep & upon waking)

Thank you for my unique gifts —

_____.

Thank you that I'm passionate about

_____.

I use my gifts, talents & passions for the common good, building up my family & my community.

Dream Goal: I see myself

_____.

I see myself

_____.

I am

_____.

I am

_____.

I am

_____.

I am

_____.

To God (or Higher Power): I can do all things through your strength. All things are possible for me when I ask, believe & take action. Please bring these into my reality or change the desires of my heart. Strengthen me to become who I am meant to be and step into my destiny.

I am my Best ME! Thank you for blessing me abundantly. I love & trust you completely.

Footnote References:

[1] In this body of work, the term "manifest" or "manifesting" means for something to appear, become apparent or come into a state of reality or being. How this happens is discussed in detail throughout the text.

[2] Our family appeared on the ABC Network hit Reality TV show "Wife Swap" in primetime on May 7, 2010. It is referred to as the "Beauvais/Clayton" episode. It will re-run on ABC and/or Lifetime Network for an unspecified period, possibly through 2014. It will also be broadcast around the world, because the program airs in 21 countries.

[3] Hebrews 12:1

[4] Proverbs 23:7 KJV

[5] Proverbs 29:18 KJV

[6] Matthew 7:7

[7] Prayer and/or meditation are considered synonymous in this practice. If you are uncomfortable with the idea of prayer, then consider quiet focused thought or other forms of meditation for this Key.

[8] To be clear, we are not talking about sleep-dreams, but the "dreams" of your heart and mind. Dreams, as we will refer to them, are made up of your passions, desires, visions, goals and aspirations. They are deep, strong and burn with passion inside of you.

[9] We define "healthy" dreams, desires or passions as those that are not self-indulgent, destructive, vain or totally self-serving in nature. For example, if a person's desire is numerous or unlimited sexual partners, we would describe this as "unhealthy." Other examples might be a desire for exorbitant wealth, greed, extreme vanity, and most other selfishly focused pursuits.

[10] Mark 9:23

[11] Mark 10:27

[12] Whitney Houston, "When You Believe" 1985©

[13] Matthew 25:21,23,29; Luke 19:17,19,26

[14] Definitions courtesy of Dictionary.com

[15] Romans 12:6, 1 Corinthians 12:7

[16] Matthew 25:14-30

[17] Please see "Success" section in the Foreword for further details.

[18] 1 Timothy 6:10

[19] Ecclesiastes 5:10-11

[20] Proverbs 29:18 NAS, ESV

[21] Visit Mellow Mushroom in Phoenix, AZ www.MellowMushroom.com/Phoenix

[22] From *Breaking the Jewish Code*, by Perry Stone

[23] 1 Corinthians 3:16-17. We should respect and take care of our body, which is a temple of the Holy Spirit.

[24] 2 Chronicles 16:9

[25] Jeremiah 29:11

[26] Matthew 7:9-11

[27] Matthew 18:4

[28] Jeremiah 29:11, Acts 17:27

[29] Psalm 145:9

[30] Hebrews 12:5-11

[31] 1 Samuel 13:14

[32] Mark 12: 30

[33] Psalm 55:22, 1 Peter 5:7

[34] Ezekiel 36:26, Ps 51:10

[35] Ephesians 4:29

[36] Mt 18:15-17, 5:25

[37] Malachi 3.10

[38] Ephesians 3:16-20

[39] John 14:23

[40] Romans 8:28

[41] Psalm 37:4

[42] Matthew 7:7-11

[43] Proverbs 16:24

[44] Proverbs 18:21

[45] James 3:6

[46] James 1:26

[47] *Hidden Messages in Water*, Dr. Masaru Emoto.

[48] Ephesians 4:29

[49] Philippians 4:8

[50] Matthew 7:12

[51] I pray out loud through my Key Cards, then visualize as I meditate on them. If you like, you can read yours out loud and meditate on them. It's your choice.

[52] The Parable of the Persistent Widow, Luke 18:1-8

[53] For the purpose of our discussion here, the "mind" and "brain" will be used synonymously, recognizing that the brain is the physical form and the mind the enigmatic form of human cognitive and reasoning abilities.

[54] Richard L. Strauss makes this point beautifully in his book *Win the Battle For Your Mind*.

[55] Genesis 1:27

[56] This will not be a deeply scientific discussion of the subject on brain/mind function, but a general layman's discussion based on well understood and established scientific facts.

[57] Matthew 19:26, Mark 10:27, Luke 18:27

[58] Mark 11:23-24

[59] *Miracle of Mind Dynamics* by Dr. Joseph Murphy

[60] Matthew 9:8 (NKJV)

[61] 2 Corinthians 10:5, Philippians 4:8

[62] Matthew 25:14-30, The Parable of the Talents

[63] A "talent" was a unit of measure, usually for gold or silver, equaling approximately 75 pounds. At today's value, a talent of gold would be worth over $1.38 Million; a talent of silver would be worth over $22,000 (Apr14.2010 Gold = $1155.40/oz, Silver = $18.40/oz).

[64] Source for "Brainwave Facts," Dr. Laura De Giorgio, Ph.D, Clinical Hypnotherapist and Mindpowercoach.com.

[65] "The Nature of Thought Energy" by Dr. Jeffry R. Palmer PhD, Project Sanctuary study, 1993.

[66] The game is made by Hammacher Schlemmer and is called Mind Flex. You can see a link to their website on our Facebook fan page: www.facebook.com/mydreamprogram.

[67] From *The Secret of the Ages* by Robert Collier

[68] Matthew 7:7-8

[69] This concept was introduced and defined by legendary author **Napoleon Hill** in the classic work *Think and Grow Rich*, originally published in 1935.

[70] In Napoleon Hill's teaching on conscious auto-suggestion, he recommended that the affirmations be repeated in the morning upon waking and at night before retiring, just as we do in the Dream Program.

[71] John 14:12

[72] Ecclesiastes 5:10

[73] Psalm 37:4, Jeremiah 29:11, Ephesians 3:21

[74] See our blog on "Mastermind Groups" at www.DreamProgram.com/blog-mastermind-groups for more on this concept.

[75] For details on Dream Program coaching please visit the "Store" page our website at www.DreamProgram.com/store.

[76] Network Marketing, or multi-level marketing as some call it, is what we are referring to here. There are many excellent companies and product types to choose from virtually anywhere, around the world. If you are hungry for such an opportunity, you will definitely be able to find one that is right for you. You must be able to get behind the product and the company with all your heart.

[77] Psalm 145:17

[78] Hosea 11:9

[79] 2 Peter 3:9, 1 Timothy 2:4

[80] Jeremiah 29:11

[81] Matthew 19:26

[82] Matthew 21:21-22

[83] John 14:10,11

[84] John 14: 12

[85] Matthew 17:20

[86] 2 Corinthians 4:7

[87] Philippians 2:13

[88] James 2:18,20

[89] 1 John 5:14-15

[90] *In Tune With The Infinite*, Ralph Waldo Trine, 1897

[91] Matthew 7:11

[92] Mark 11:22-24

[93] This thought on 'discouragement' is adapted from Robert Collier's work, *The Secret of The Ages*.

[94] Matthew 6:25-34

[95] Psalm 37:4

[96] *Dream to Destiny*, by Rob Kenney © 2001; used by permission

[97] Deuteronomy 30:11-14

[98] Luke 17:21

[99] The Parable of the Talents/Ten Minas – Matthew 25:14-30, Luke 19:11-27

[100] A "talent" was a unit of measure equaling approximately 75 lbs. Five talents of gold at today's value would be worth over $6.93 Million. Five talents of silver at today's value would be worth over $110,000. (Apr14.2010 Gold = $1155.40/oz, Silver = $18.40/oz)

[101] Matthew 18:3

[102] James 1:6

[103] Placing the "Career" priority after friends/neighbors emphasizes the point that people are more important than money, "success" or things. The Dream Program acknowledges that career often commands a dominant time commitment in your life. Career may even call for an emotional commitment in some circumstances. However from a "heart" or "love" standpoint we believe that people should come before career in terms of life priorities.

[104] Matthew 7:24-27, Luke 6:46-49

[105] Jeremiah 29:13, Acts 17:27

[106] Philippians 2:1-11, Romans 8:29

[107] John 14:6, Mark 10:27, 9:23

[108] Romans 8:37,31

[109] *Evidence That Demands A Verdict*, by Josh McDowell, 1999; *The Case For Christ*, by Lee Strobel, 1998; *True & Reasonable*, by Dr. Douglas Jacoby, 1999

[110] John 14:27 NLT

[111] Isaiah 26:3 TNIV

[112] James 4:10, 1 Peter 5:10

[113] James 2:16,18

[114] Philippians 4:7

[115] Matthew 8:26, Mark 4:40

[116] 1 John 4:16,18

[117] Jeremiah 29:11

[118] Ephesians 3:20

[119] Steven Covey, from *The 7 Habits of Highly Effective People*.

[120] Philippians 4:8

[121] Matthew 7:11

[122] Matthew 7:7-8

[123] Matthew 9:29

[124] Matthew 21:18-22

[125] Matthew 13:58

[126] Psalm 37:4

[127] 1 Corinthians 3:5-9

[128] Ephesians 3:20

Made in the USA
Lexington, KY
23 February 2012